The Architectural History
of
Winchester Cathedral

by

The Reverend R. Willis M.A., F.R.S.
Jacksonian Professor of the University of Cambridge

D0942953

The Friends of Winchester Cathedral
The Close, Winchester
1984
(Reprinted 1992)

Printed by Culverlands Press Ltd, Winchester, Hampshire.

Preface

No student of the architecture of Winchester Cathedral can pursue his studies very far before he comes across the name of Robert Willis, whose *History of the Architecture of Winchester Cathedral*, first written in 1845, has never been outdated and which still tops the list of required reading for anyone wishing to make a serious study of the subject. Unfortunately, however, Willis' paper has not been easy to obtain. It forms a part of the "Proceedings at the Annual Meeting of the Archaeological Institute of Great Britain and Ireland, at Winchester, September, MDCCCXLV", to give the volume its full title, but this, while available for reference in a small number of select public and academic libraries, is only to be found very occasionally in the second-hand bookshops. In 1972 a collection of Robert Willis' architectural papers, including his history of Winchester Cathedral, was published in two volumes by Paul Minet, at the suggestion of Sir Nikolaus Pevsner, under the title *Architectural History of Some English Cathedrals*, but the volume containing the Winchester paper is now out of print. In making Willis' History obtainable in a new and handy form the Friends of the Cathedral therefore believe that they are doing a service that will be widely appreciated.

Robert Willis was born in 1800 and "when a mere lad" to quote his biographer (J. Willis Clark) in the *Dictionary of National Biography*, "he was a skilful musician, a good draughtsman and an eager examiner of every piece of machinery and ancient building that came his way". He was ordained in 1827 and was elected Fellow of Gonville and Caius College two years later. In 1837 he became Jacksonian Professor of Applied Mechanics at Cambridge.

Willis quickly appreciated the affinity between mechanical engineering and architecture. To quote his biographer again, "He treated a building as he treated a machine: he took it to pieces; he pointed out what was structural and what was decorative, what was imitated and what was original; and how the most complex forms of mediaeval invention might be reduced to simple elements." This method of analysis soon developed into particular studies that combined practical architecture with antiquarian research.

Willis himself described his method of approach in the preamble to his Winchester paper, and it is well illustrated by his opening chapter in which he gathers together with scrupulous care all the historical evidence that might have a bearing on his theme.

The paper was presented to the Archaeological Institute at its first meeting, which was held at Winchester in September 1845 in St. John's Rooms. There was a distinguished gathering. The president of the Institute, the Marquis of Northampton, took the chair, and among the opening speakers were the Dean of Winchester, the Dean of Westminster, the Master of Trinity College, Cambridge, the Warden of New College and the Master of University College. Professor Willis presented his paper on the following morning, and in the afternoon he "accompanied a large party to the Cathedral, and illustrated his lecture by directing attention to various parts of the building, pointing out the grounds of his deductions, and showing the method of his researches in a manner most gratifying to those who accompanied him".

Today's readers can have no less reason than Robert Willis' original audience for their gratification, for they will find that he speaks with his pen almost as vividly as he could have done with his voice.

Note

This Preface is an amended copy of the Preface written for the earlier edition of this work published by the Friends of the Cathedral in 1980, when it appeared in company with Professor Christopher Brooke's essay "The Normans as Cathedral Builders".

Professor Robert Willis addressing the Archaeological Institute at Winchester.
September 1845.
(from an engraving in the Illustrated London News)

PROCEEDINGS

AT THE ANNUAL MEETING

OF THE

𝕬𝖗𝖈𝖍𝖆𝖊𝖔𝖑𝖔𝖌𝖎𝖈𝖆𝖑 𝕴𝖓𝖘𝖙𝖎𝖙𝖚𝖙𝖊

OF GREAT BRITAIN AND IRELAND,

AT WINCHESTER, SEPTEMBER, MDCCCXLV.

LONDON:

LONGMAN, BROWN, GREEN, AND LONGMANS;

W. PICKERING, PICCADILLY; G. BELL, FLEET STREET.

OXFORD: J. H. PARKER.—CAMBRIDGE: J. AND J. J. DEIGHTON.

WINCHESTER: JACOB AND JOHNSON.

M DCCC XLVI.

THE ARCHITECTURAL HISTORY OF WINCHESTER CATHEDRAL.

BY THE REV. R. WILLIS, M.A., F.R.S., &c.

JACKSONIAN PROFESSOR OF THE UNIVERSITY OF CAMBRIDGE.

IN this history I propose to follow the same plan which I adopted with respect to Canterbury Cathedral, namely, to bring together all the recorded evidence that belongs to the building, excluding historical matter that relates only to the see or district; to examine the building itself for the purpose of investigating the mode of its construction, and the successive changes and additions that have been made to it; and lastly, to compare the recorded evidence with the structural evidence as much as possible. A complete delineation and description of the building must not be expected, any more than a complete history of the see. The first have been most admirably supplied in the plates and text of Mr. Britton's well known volume, and the able and copious work of Milner contains every particular that can be required for the second. But still it appeared to me that the history of the building might be disentangled with advantage from the mass of local information in which it is enveloped in these works, and that the present advanced state of archæological knowledge in architecture called for a closer investigation of the structure than had hitherto been attempted. Unfortunately, no Gervase has recorded this history of the cathedral, and we can only pick out detached fragments of written evidence.

The principal sources are, Rudborne's " Historia Major," and the " Annales Ecclesiæ Wintoniensis," both printed by Wharton. There exists also in the Library of All Souls College, Oxford, a manuscript chronicle of the church of St. Swithun at Winchester, by John of Exeter. By the kindness of the Rev. Lewis Sneyd, M.A., Warden of All Souls College, the Institute has been furnished with a transcript of this chronicle, of which

I have availed myself in the following pages. The title of the manuscript sets forth[a] that John of Exeter wrote it with his own hands in the year of our Lord 1531. But at the end of it is a list of kings of England, with the dates of their coronations, deaths, and places of burial. This list concludes with the coronation of Henry the Sixth in 1421, and with a prayer for his prosperity. Also our author's list of the bishops terminates with the succession of Cardinal Beaufort. As he died in 1447, during the reign of Henry the Sixth, we may conclude the manuscript to have been written between 1421 and 1447, and, therefore, that the date at the beginning must be read 1431 instead of 1531.

The manuscript which Wharton calls an Epitome of Rudborne, and which in his time existed in the Cottonian Library, (Galba A 15), but was unhappily burnt, appears to have been the same with this work of John of Exeter. It begins with the same words[b], and contains the list of bishops, of which Wharton has printed the latter part at the end of his copy of Rudborne (p. 285). But it is ill described as an epitome, for, although in common with Rudborne, the early part of the history is made up of extracts from the lost works of Moracius, Vigilantius, &c., yet these extracts are often more copious than Rudborne's, and many particulars are thus supplied, as well as in the latter periods, which especially relate to the burial places of the bishops and kings.

Other sources of information are contained in the Life of Ethelwold, by Wolstan[c], and similar works. And for William of Wykeham, the admirable biography by Bishop Louth supplies every kind of documental information.

In conclusion, I beg to express my thanks to the dean and chapter of the cathedral, for the kind and hospitable facilities which enabled me to carry on the investigations which form the subject of the following pages.

[a] The title is as follows: " Liber historialis et antiquitatum domus Sancti Swithuni Wintoniæ Johannis Exceter ejusdem loci commonachi propriis manibus descriptus, anno dominice Incarnationis millesimo quingentesimo tricesimo primo." The manuscript concludes with the words, " Hec Exceter propria scripsit manu. Finis." It does not follow that this manuscript is an autograph, and the clerical error in the date seems to shew that it is not.

[b] " Tempore quo humanæ salutis," &c. Ang. Sac. p. 179.

[c] Acta Sanctorum Ordinis S. Benedicti Sæc. V.

CHAP. I.

THE HISTORY OF THE CATHEDRAL TO THE YEAR 1170.

1. EARLY tradition has carried the history of this church far higher than that of Canterbury, for we are told that Lucius, king of the Britons, after his conversion to Christianity, (c. A.D. 164,) did erect from the foundations (or rather rebuild in lieu of a previous temple) the church of the British town of Kaergwent (now called Winchester or Winton). Also that he placed monks there, and erected for their temporary accommodation a small dwelling, with an oratory, refectory and dormitory, until the great work should be completed[a].

This having been effected in the fifth year of the king's conversion, the church was dedicated in honour of the holy Saviour, on the fourth kalend of November, A.D. 169, and endowed with the possessions that had formerly belonged to the pagan priests. The dimensions of this church are stated, on the authority of the lost work of the British historian Moracius[b], to have been 209 passus in length, 80 in breadth, and 92 in altitude. From one extremity of the church across to the other was 180 passus[c].

The site of the monastery to the east of the church was 100 passus in length towards the old temple of Concord, and 40 in breadth towards the new temple of Apollo. The north portion was 160 in length, and 98 in breadth. To the west of the church it was 190 in length, and 100 in breadth. To the south 405 in length, and 580 in breadth. On this side was placed the episcopal palace and the offices of the monks[d].

2. During the persecution of Diocletian[e], A.D. 266, the monastery of Winchester was destroyed, and reconstructed by the assistance of the oblations of the faithful, in the year

[a] Rudborne, (Ang. Sac., v. 1, p. 181,) on the authority of the lost work of Vigilantius, " de basilica Petri," i. e. on the church of St. Peter at Wynton. This work is quoted perpetually by Rudborne and John of Exeter, and appears to have been the principal local history. The quotations terminate immediately before the Conquest, to which period therefore we may refer the author in question.

[b] " Ille antiquus Britannorum conscriptor Moracius."—Rudborne, p. 182.

[c] In the All Souls manuscript of John of

Exeter these dimensions are stated somewhat differently, (still quoting Moracius,) as 200 pass. in length, and 130 across; the rest coincide.

[d] " In hac plaga situatum est palatium episcopale, domus necessariæ, ac officinæ monachorum."—Rudborne, p. 185. I leave to others the task of reducing these measurements to consistency with each other and with probability. Perhaps by reading *pedes* for *passus*, one foot for five, we may assist in this work.

[e] Rudborne, 183.

293, when it was dedicated in honour of St. Amphibalus, one of those who suffered under the late persecution. But this church was neither so large as the former, nor was the monastery so extensive as that of King Lucius. From this time it bore the name of the old monastery, "Vetus Cœnobium[f]." When the Saxons obtained the rule over the land, Cerdic, the first king of the west, was crowned at Winchester, and having slain the monks, converted the church of St. Amphibalus into a temple of Dagon, in the year 516 [g].

3. Thus it remained for one hundred and forty-two years, until the advent of St. Birinus, the first apostle of the west, who, by the mission of Pope Honorius, came to these regions forty-one years after the coming of St. Augustine, namely, in the year 635, and converted the king Kynegils and all his people to Christianity[h].

This king having destroyed the temple of Dagon which Cerdic had erected, began the foundation of the cathedral church of Winchester, which he was prevented by death from completing[i]. But he granted the whole of the land for the space of seven miles round the city for the establishment of the episcopal seat, and for the maintenance of the monks, who were now, by the advice of Birinus, for the third time esta-

[f] Rudborne, 186.
[g] Rudborne, 187.
[h] MS. John of Exeter, f. 2, 6; Rudborne, 189, &c.
[i] " In votis enim ejus erat in Wintonia ædificare templum præcipuum et collectis jam plurimis ad opus ædificii terram totam ambientem Wintoniam à centro Wintoniæ usque ad circumferentiam ab omni parte lineâ exeunte septem leucas habentem ædificandæ ecclesiæ in dotem dare disposuit. Quæ quia letiferâ præventus ægritudine per se complere non potuit ; vicario usus est ; vocatumque ad se filium suum Kinewalchum fecit jurare coram S. Birino in animam suam quod ipse ecclesiam sede episcopali dignam construeret in Wintonia et terram quam circinaveret, eidem ecclesiæ ad opus ministeriorum ejus ex parte suâ Deo offeret et in jus perpetuum confirmaret. A°. DCXXXIX Kinewalchus filius Kinegilsi. Iste post vexationes quas pertulit a Pendâ rege Merciorum propter repudium filiæ suæ, ecclesiam pulcherrimam construxit in Wyntonia et totam terram quam pater voverat ecclesia contulit et confirmavit."—Annales Wint. Ang. Sac., p. 288.
" Kynegilsus primus occidentalium rex Christianus incepit fundare ecclesiam cathedralem Wintonie, ut ibi gloriosus posset primas Anglie et Gewyseorum apostolus primus almifluus pontifex Birinus pontificalibus insigniri infulis. Sed morte invalescente opus inceptum non potuit perficere sed assignata terra tota in circuitu civitatis ad spacium septem miliariorum ad constructionem sedis episcopalis et ad sustentationem monachorum quos ex consilio sancti Birini terna vice introduxit sub protestatione juramenti a filio suo Kinewaldo soluta in speciali pro parte testamenti suo legavit heredi. Sicque regni sui negociis per omnia rite dispositis spiritum comendavit in manus Creatoris anno regni sui xxxi, conversionis vero sue anno sexto, pontificatus beatissimi patris Birini anno vi et in Wentana civitate in ipsa ecclesia quam edificare inceperat coram summo altari corpus ejus traditur sepulture. Kynewaldus patri in regnum succedens paternum propositum summo preceptum quam studiosius potuit adimplevit, perfectaque fabrica ecclesie Wentane que modo vetus nominatur cenobium sanctificataque cetu monachorum conveniente, dedicavit ipsam basilicam Christi summusta Birinus summe ac individue Trinitatis honore."—John of Exeter MS. f. 2, b. See also Rudborne, pp. 189, 190, &c.

blished in this place. And having bound his son Kynewald by an oath to complete his intentions, he died in the thirty-first year of his reign, and in the sixth of his conversion, and was buried in the city of Winchester, before the high altar of the church which he had begun to build.

Kynewald succeeded to his father's crown, and completed the fabric of the church of Winchester. In the sixth year of his reign Birinus dedicated this basilica of Christ in honour of the holy and indivisible Trinity.

4. Meanwhile the seat of the episcopal government had been temporarily established at Dorchester, in Oxfordshire, by King Kynegils, waiting the completion of the works at Winchester, and at Dorchester the body of Birinus was first deposited. But when Hedda, the fourth successor of Birinus in the episcopate, removed the episcopal seat to Winchester in accordance with the original intention of the royal founder, the body of Birinus was translated thither.

5. King Kynewald, the completor of the fabric, was buried before (or under) the high altar [j]. And of the succeeding bishops of Winchester it is recorded that the following were buried there[k]. Hedda—"Humfredus and Kinehardus were both buried in the north part of the church in the crypt, as Vigilancius writeth." "Egbladus, Dud and Kynebrithus, all three, lie inhumed in the crypt, under the altar of the Virgin Mary; and Almundus, Wyderginnus, Herforthus, and Edmundus in the nave of the church; Edmundus near the door of the choir, as Vigilancius recordeth." "Helmstanus was buried before the high altar, but since in a leaden coffin deposited on the north side of the altar, over the tomb of Bishop Richard Toklyn[l]."

6. St. Swithun was made bishop of Winchester in the year 852, having previously held the office of prior in that church. He was a diligent builder of churches in places where there were none before, and repaired those that had been destroyed

[j] "Kynewaldus, filius Kyngelsi qui opus ecclesie a patre inceptum complevit et tria maneria eidem ecclesia dedit . . . qui sepultus est sub summo altare."—John of Exeter, f. 5, b; also Rudb., p. 191.

[k] "Hedda . . . Wintonie sepultus est . . . . Humfridus et Kinehardus ambo sepulti sunt Wintonie in boreali parte ecclesie sub cripta ut scribit Vigilancius . . . . . Egbladus, Dud, Kynebirthus, Almundus, Wydergynnus, Herforthus, Edmundus. Quo-

rum tres primi jacent humati in cripta sub Dei genetricis altari; quatuor secundi in navi ecclesie, Edmundus jacet prope ostium chori, ut scribit Vigilantius . . . . Helmstano in ecclesia Wintoniensi sepulto coram summo altari sed modo in locello plumbeo posito ex boreali plaga altaris supra tumulum Richardi Toklyn episcopi."—John of Exeter, f. 3, b.

[l] This bishop filled the see from 1174 to 1189.

or ruined. He also built a bridge on the east side of the city, and during the work he made a practice of sitting there to watch the workmen, that his presence might stimulate their industry[m]. He died in the year 863, and was buried, in accordance to his own injunctions, outside the church, in a vile and unworthy place, where his grave was trampled on by every passenger, and received the droppings from the eaves. Afterwards a small and beautiful chapel was erected there to his honour, which, says Rudborne, is still to be seen at the north door of the nave of the church[n].

Wolstan, describing the place in his metrical eulogium of the saint, says[o], that a tower, capped with a roof, and of the greatest magnitude, stood before the lovely entrance of the holy temple. Between this and the sacred nave (aula) of the temple, the body of the saint was interred. And he adds, that out of his extreme humility, he not only thought himself unworthy to be deposited within the church, but that he would not even lie amongst the other graves that received the rays of the rising sun and the noonday warmth, for he commanded his body to be deposited on the western side of that famous nave.

[m] " Sanctus iste ecclesias in locis in quibus non erant studiose fabricavit dirutas et fractas reparavit . . . . . Hic etiam sanctum po..tem ad orientem Wintonie construxit." —Capgrave. " Operariis ad pontem in orientali parte urbis faciendum forte assederat, ut instanti presentia suscitaret stimulos desidum incuriæ."—W. Malm., 242.

[n] " Præcepit ut extra ecclesiam cadaver suum humarent: ubi et pedibus prætereuntium et stillicidiis ex alto rorantibus esset obnoxium."—W. Malm., de gest. Pont., p. 242.

" Extra ecclesiam in indigno loco et vili."—Capgrave.

" Jam verò valefacturus cadaver suum extra ecclesiam præcepit tumulari ubi postea constructa est modica capella, quæ adhuc cernitur ad boreale ostium navis ecclesiæ."—Rudborne, 203. " S. Swithunus . . . . sepultus est extra portam borealem navis ecclesie qui locus tunc indecens erat, modo vero ibidem quam pulchra capella in ejus honore constructa est."—John of Exeter, f. 4.

[o] Turris erat rostrata tholis, quia maxima quædam,
Illius ante sacri pulcherrima limina templi,
Ejusdem sacrata Deo sub honore hierarchi.
Inter quam, templique sacram pernobilis aulam,
Corpore vir Domini sanctus requievit humatus, &c.
. . . .
Mente humili in tantum presul fuit inclitus idem,
Ut perhibent omnes, hunc qui novêre fideles,
Ut se post obitum sineret nullatenus intra
Ecclesiæ Christi penetralia corpore poni:
Sed nec in electis loca per diversa sepulcris,
In quibus antiqui patres jacuêre sepulti,
Aurea sol oriens orbi qua spicula mittit,
Qua mediumque diem fervente calore perurit:
Sed magis occiduo mandat se climate poni
Illius illustris, quam sæpe notavimus, aulæ.
     Wolstan. Vit. S. Swithuni, Act. Sanc. Jul., tom. i. 321.

7. Two years after the death of Swithun, the Danes entered and ravaged Winchester, and slew the whole of the monks, but the cathedral is not said to have suffered. Tumbertus, however, the second bishop after Swithun, gave the manor of Stusheling to the fabric of the church[p]. Bishops Frithestanus and Brinstanus were both buried in the north aisle of the church, and Elphegus on the north side of the high altar[q].

8. Bishop Athelwold was too great a promoter of ecclesiastical architecture to be dismissed with a summary notice. He, while a monk at Winchester, having by his piety recommended himself to Edgiva, queen of Edward the Elder, and mother of the reigning king Eadred, was by him appointed to the abbacy of Abingdon, a place where of old a small monastery had been established, but which was now deserted. There, however, the king was desirous of founding a new monastery, which he and his mother richly endowed. "And the king himself came on a certain day to this monastery to give orders and arrange the structure of the buildings; with his own hands he measured all the foundations, and himself commanded in what manner the walls should be made; when this was done the abbot requested him to dine in his hospitium. And the king, in the joy of his heart, sat down with a large party of his nobles from Northumberland, who happened to be with him. He called for abundance of hydromel, and, having locked the doors, lest any of the party should evade their due share of the royal potations, they drank merrily till the evening[r]." "Nevertheless, the abbot did not begin to erect the projected works in the days of King Eadred, for that king

---

[p] Rudborne, p. 206.

[q] " S. Frithesthanus .... S. Brithestanus ... qui ambo in aquilonari ala ecclesie Wentone honorifice traduntur sepulturæ. Tunc Elphegus confessor ...... ad aquilonarem plagam summi altaris corpus ejus veneratione dignum humatum est."—John of Exeter, f. 4.

[r] "Venit Rex quadam die ad Monasterium ut ædificiorum structuram per se ipsum ordinaret: mensusque omnia fundamenta Monasterii propria manu, quemadmodum muros erigere decreverat, rogavitque eum Abbas in hospitio cum suis prandere. Annuit Rex ilico, et contigit adesse sibi non paucos Optimatum suorum venientes ex gente Nordamhimbrorum, qui omnes Rege adierunt convivium. Lætatusque Rex et jussit abunde propinare hospitibus hydromellum, clausis diligenter foribus

ne quis fugiendo potationem regalis convivi, deserere videretur. Quid multa? hauserunt ministri liquorem tota die ad omnem sufficientiam convivantibus; sed nequivit ipse liquor exhauriri de vase nisi ad mensuram palmi in ebrietate suatim Nordanhimbris et vesperi cum lætitia recedentibus."—Wolstan. Vit. S. Ethel., p. 613. Many of the anecdotes that follow, I have translated from the Life of Athelwold, (or Ethelwold), which Mabillon has printed in the fifth volume of the " Acta Sanctorum Ordini S. Benedicti." He identifies with apparent reason this biography with that mentioned by William of Malmsbury, who speaking of Bishop Ethelwold, says that his life was written in a somewhat indifferent style by his pupil Wolstan, cantor of Winton. Mabillon. A. S. p. 606.

was suddenly removed from this life on the ninth kalend of December. But during the reign of his glorious son and successor Eadgar, the abbot completed an honourable temple dedicated to the Virgin Mary[s]."

9. "King Eadred proved himself an especial admirer and friend of the 'old cenobium' of Winchester—witness the ornaments which were by his orders made for that place; a golden cross, a golden altar, and many others, which, with a liberal hand, he there bestowed in honour of the blessed Apostles Peter and Paul. Had he lived he intended to have adorned the eastern apse of the church of Winchester with gilded tiles[t]."

10. "The holy Athelwold was a great builder of churches, and of various other works, both while he was abbot, and after he became bishop of Winchester," and, like his friend and cotemporary Dunstan, was himself a workman. "Hence the malignity of the adversary endeavoured to compass his destruction; for, on a certain day, when the holy man was working at construction, a great post fell upon him and knocked him into a pit, breaking nearly all his ribs on one side, so that, had it not been for the pit, he would have been crushed to pieces[u]."

After this he was elected by King Eadgar to the episcopate of Winchester, and consecrated there in the year 963.

11. "At Winton he repaired and endowed a monastery of nuns, originally founded by Ethelswytha, mother of Edward the Elder, in honour of the Blessed Virgin. He purchased, and for no small sum, a certain spot called Ely, where there had been originally a monastery of Etheldreda, Saint and Virgin, which, having been destroyed by the Danes, the place had become royal property. Here he established monks, and

---

[s] Wolstan. Vit. S. Ethel. p. 613.

[t] ". . . Eadredus erat Veteris cenobii in Wintonia specialis amator atque defensor, ut testantur ea quæ ipso jubente fabricata sunt ornamenta magna scilicet aurea crux, altare aureum et cetera quæ larga manu benignus illuc ad honorem beatorum Apostolorum Petri et Pauli direxit ibique æternaliter ad Dei laudem et gloriam conservari precepit qui etiam, si vita comes fieret, orientalem porticum ejusdem Wintoniensis ecclesiæ deauratis imbricibus adornare disposuit."—Wolstani Vita S. Ethelwoldi. Mab., tom. v. p. 612.

[u] "Erat . . sanctus Athelwoldus ecclesiarum ac diversorum operum, magnus ædificator et dum esset Abbas et dum esset Episcopus. Unde tetendit ei communis adversarius solitas suæ malignitatis insidias, ut eum, si ullo modo posset extingueret. Nam quadam die dum vir Dei in structura laboraret, ingens postis super eum cecidit, et in quandam foveam dejecit confregitque pœne omnes costas ejus ex uno latere, ita ut nisi fovea illum susciperet, totus quassaretur."—Wolstan. 614.

"Nescires quid in eo magis laudares : sanctitatis studium, an doctrinarum exercitium, in prædicatione instantiam, in ædificiis industriam."—W. Malmsb. p. 244.

instituted Brythnothus, the prepositus of the old monastery of Wynton, abbot, erecting buildings there. Also he bought of King Edgar a place then called Medamstede, but since named Burgh[v]. Here he consecrated a basilica, in honour of St. Peter, furnished with all its proper edifices, and established monks there, with Eadulphus for their abbot, who afterwards succeeded St. Oswald as archbishop of York. Thirdly, and at no less expense, he acquired a place, which, from the abundance of briars that grew about it, was called Thorneia; and there he established monks, with Godmannus for their abbot, about the year of grace 970, as it is recorded by Johannes in his Históriâ Aureâ[x]."

12. "In the days of King Edgar the holy father Athelwold translated the blessed Birinus, the first apostle of the west, and placed him in a comely *scrinium,* made of silver and gold: for when St. Hedda, bishop of Winchester, removed the body of the holy father Birinus from Dorchester, he buried it in the church of Winchester, on the north side of the high altar, and it was not translated 'more sanctorum' until the time of Athelwold, as Vigilancius writeth, and as it is also said in the legend which is read in the church of Winchester on the octave of the translation of St. Birinus. Moreover, after Athelwold had, with the consent of King Edgar, expelled the canons and replaced them with monks, he, admonished by a divine revelation, removed St. Swithun, the especial patron of the church of Winton, from his mean sepulchre, and placed him with all honour in a 'scrinium' of gold and silver, of the richest workmanship, the gift of King Edgar.

"The saint was thus translated in the hundred and tenth year of his rest. And for his glory, so great was the concourse of people, and so numerous and frequent the miracles, that the like had never been witnessed in England; for so long as the canons inhabited the church of Winchester, St. Swithun performed no miracles, but the moment they were ejected the miracles began, as Vigilancius testifieth, and also Lantfredus. St. Athelwold also translated the bodies of Saints Frythestane, Brinstan, and Elphege, together with the holy virgin Edburga, daughter of Edward the Elder[y]."

13. "When the holy man had earnestly set about the re-

[v] Now Peterborough.
[x] Translated from Rudborne, p. 218.
See also Wolstan, p. 615.

[y] Translated from Rudborne, p. 223.
See also John of Exeter, f. 4.

building of the old church (of Winchester), he commanded the brethren to assist in the works, together with the artificers and workmen. Thus the labourers emulating one another the building gradually rose aloft, sustained on every side by many oratories intended for those who would ask help from the saints. It happened one day, while the brethren were standing with the masons at the very top of the temple, that one of them, by name Godus, fell from the highest point to the ground, but he immediately arose unhurt, and when he had crossed himself and wondered how he came there, he ascended in sight of the spectators to the place he had left, and taking up his trowel went on with his work[z]."

14. In the year of the Lord 980, and on the 13th kalend of November (Oct. 20,) the church of the old cenobium at Wynton was dedicated by nine bishops, of whom the first and principal were Archbishop Dunstan, and the holy Bishop Athelwold, in presence of King Etheldred, and of nearly every duke, abbot, and noble of England[a]. The church was dedicated in honour of the Apostles Peter and Paul[b]. At this point of the history the biographer Wolstan, quitting prose, gives vent to his enthusiam in a poem, of which more below.

Athelwold died at *Beaddington*, sixty miles from Winchester, in the kalends of August, and in the year of the Incarnation 984, in the twenty-second of his episcopate, and under the reign of Ethelred. His body was conveyed to the church of the Apostles Peter and Paul at Winchester, and buried in

[z] "Cum in Dei magno conamine veterem renovare decrevisset ecclesiam jussit fratres frequenter laboribus una cum artificibus et operariis insistere, quibus certatim laborantibus, opus ædificii paullatim in sublime excrevit, plurimis hinc inde suffultum Oratoriis in quibus Sanctorum venerantur suffragia, cunctis fideliter accedentibus profutura. Contigit autem quadam die, dum fratres starent ad summum culmen templi cum cæmentariis, ut unus eorum Godus nomine, caderet à summis usque ad terram qui mox ut terram attigit, incolumis surgens stetit, nil mali passus de tanta ruina : seque crucis signaculo benedixit, admirans quid ibi ageret, vel qualiter illuc venerit. Et cunctis qui aderant videntibus ascendit ad locum ubi antea steterat et accipiens trullam, operi quod inchoaverat, diligentius insistebat. Cui ergo hoc miraculum adscribendum est, nisi illi, cujus jussu ad opus obedientiæ

exivit? qui idcirco lædi non potuit, quia hunc in casu suo viri Dei meritum portavit, et a periculo ruinæ incolumem protexit." Wolstan. p. 619.

[a] Wolstan, p. 621; and Rudborne, p. 223.

[b] " Ecclesiam Wintanam de novo renovavit criptas in ipsa ordinans dedicarique eam fecit in honore apostolorum Petri et Pauli anno primo Etheldredi regis ipso rege presente cum proceribus et ducibus tocius regni officium dedicationis dedicante Dunstano archiepiscopo cum octo episcopis anno gratiæ DCCCCLXXX sub die xiii Kalendarium Novembrium quorum nomina sunt hec ut recitat Lantfredus in libro fundamenti metro quarto. Et etiam Vigilantius in libro de Basilica Petri, cap. 14. Ipse sanctus Athelwoldus (1.) Sigericus, (2.) Elstanus, (3.) Elphegus, (4.) Erbnithus, (5.) Wlfius, (6.) Elfricus."—John of Exeter, f. 4. b.

the crypt on the south side of the holy altar[c]. But twelve years afterwards, his successor Elphege (the same who became archbishop of Canterbury, and was slain by the Danes) was induced, by miracles, to translate the body of Athelwold, and place it in the choir of the church. This was performed on the fourth idus of September [d].

15. The poetical description which Wolstan has given us of the church and monastery of Winchester at this period is so curious, that it will be necessary to analyse it, and translate those portions that really afford information of the kind that may be useful for our present purpose. The greatest part of it consists of inflated and pompous expatiation upon the wondrous qualities of the work, or of the persons engaged upon it. About seventy lines of it occur in the life of St. Athelwold. But the entire work is a poem of three hundred and thirty lines, in the form of an epistle to the Bishop Elphege, who succeeded to St. Athelwold. As the work of a cotemporary writer its information is highly valuable[e].

16. The poem opens with a long exordium addressed to the Bishop Elphege, in which, after telling him how highly the monastery is graced by his worth, and exalted by the various ornaments which he has bestowed upon it within and without, it proceeds to state that the said monastery had been rebuilt or renovated by his predecessor Athelwold :—

" He built all these dwelling places with strong walls. He covered them with roofs, and clothed them with beauty. He brought hither sweet floods of water abounding with fish ; the runnings off of the pond penetrate all the recesses of the buildings, and gently murmuring cleanse the whole cenobium[f].

" He repaired the courts (atria) of that old temple with lofty walls and

[c] " Sepultus est in crypta ad australem plagam sancti altaris." (Wolstan, p. 623.) " . . . . . summi altaris." (John of Exeter, f. 4. b.)

[d] Wolstan, p. 624. See also Rudborne, p. 223 ; and Malmsb. de gest. Pont., p. 245.

[e] The poem in its first form is printed in Wolstan's Life of St. Ethelwold, by Mabillon, (A. S[m]. Ord[s]. Ben., tom. v. p. 621), and in its complete form in the same volume, p. 628. There is a manuscript copy of the latter in the British Museum. Bib. Reg. 15. c. vii. p. 243. Plut. xvi. G.

[f] Milner quotes these lines of Wolstan on the aqueduct, and adds the following quotation from Richardson's edition of Godwin, " de Presulibus Angliæ." This editor

had the use of some manuscript notes of Antony Wood, who unfortunately does not quote his authorities, although it appears from coincident passages that he employed the All Souls manuscript of John of Exeter. " In tantum dilexit (Athelwoldus) urbem Wentanam, quod aquam currentem suo studio et labore sumptibusque largifluis benignissime introduxit." He adds that Athelwold made different canals, one of which begins near the village of Worthy, and thus distributed the water, at great toil and expense, throughout the city, and that Wolstan's lines refer to that part of the river which is called the Lock Pond, which still runs through the close. (Milner, vol. i. p. 161.)

new roofs; and strengthened it on the north sides and on the south sides with solid aisles (porticibus) and various arches.

" He added also many chapels, with sacred altars, that distract attention from the threshold of the church, so that a stranger walking in the courts is at a loss where to turn, seeing on all sides doors open to him without any certain path. He stands with wondering eyes, fascinated with the fine roofs of the intricate structure, until some experienced guide conducts him to the portals of the farthest vestibule. Here, marvelling, he crosses himself, and knows not how to quit, so dazzling is the construction, and so brilliant the variety of the fabric that sustains this ancient church, which that devout father himself strengthened, roofed, endowed and dedicated."

About fifty lines are now given to the dedication of the church, and the prodigious feasting, the eating and drinking, which accompanied it. King Ethelred, and nine bishops, whose names are enumerated⁵, were present. In the first copy of the poem a tenth bishop, *Poca*, is added, who is said upon this occasion to have done little and drank much.

> "Et tandem decimus POCA venit Episcopus illuc
> Nulla laboris agens, pocula multa bibens."   Mab. 622.

Most of the nobility of England were present, and such a dedication had never been seen in the land as that which now was celebrated in the old monastery of St. Peter at Winton[h].

⁵ Vide note to article 17.

[h] · · · · · · · · ovans Antistes ADELUUOLD, · · · ·
Qui struxit firmis hæc cuncta habitacula muris
  Ille etiam tectis texit et ipsa novis
Et cunctis decoravit ovans id honoribus, hucque
  Dulcia piscose flumina traxit aquæ
Secessusque laci penetrant secreta domorum
  Mundantes totum murmure cœnobium.
The above lines occur only in the second form of the poem; the following are common to the two copies.
Istius antiqui reparavit et atria templi
  Mœnibus excelsis culminibusque novis.
Partibus hoc Austri firmans et partibus Arcti
  Porticibus solidis, arcubus et variis.
Addidit et plures sacris altaribus ædes
  Quæ retinent dubium liminis introitum.
Quisquis ut ignotis deambulat atria plantis
  Nesciat unde meat, quovè pedem referat
Omni parte fores quia conspiciuntur aperta
  Nec patet ulla sibi semita certa viæ
Huc illucque vagos stans circumducit ocellos
  Attica Dedalei tecta stupetque soli
Certior adveniat donec sibi ductor et ipsum
  Ducat ad extremi limina vestibuli
Hic secum mirans cruce se consignat et unde
  Exeat, attonito pectore scire nequit
Sic constructa micat sic et variata coruscat
  Machina quæ { veterem / hanc matrem } sustinet ecclesiam
Quam pater ille pius summa pietate refertus
  Nominis ad laudem celsitonantis Heri

17. With the dedication of the church the first copy of the poem (in the life of St. Athelwold) closes, but in the second copy, which, as above mentioned, is addressed in the form of an epistle to Bishop Elphege, more than two hundred lines are added in description of the works which that bishop carried on to complete his predecessor's plan.

[i]" Thus the inspired bishop (Athelwold) fulfilled before the Lord many vows. For he laid a foundation eastward, so that an apse (porticus) might there be built to the Deity. And having laid a foundation he erected a new temple, but being removed from this world was unable to complete it."
" You" (Elphege, his successor) " have diligently carried on the work commenced. Above all, you have taken care to add the secret crypts, which subtle ingenuity had so contrived, that whoever entered them for the first time would be at a loss which way to turn. Within, secret recesses lie on every side ; their outer covering is manifest, but their caves within are hidden. Their entrances and exits stand open, but a stranger looking in (from without) sees only darkness and shadow, although they really receive a borrowed light from the sun."—" Their structure supports the holy altar and the venerable relics of the saints, and in many ways their upper surface is useful, bearing things without, and covering those that are within. Moreover, you have here constructed such organs that the like were never seen."

Fulcivit, texit,		eamque	
Fundavit, struxit	dotavit	et inde.	sacravit.

In this and the former line the upper readings belong to the first form of the poem, and the lower readings to the latter form. It is remarkable that in the first, the expressions used describe the repair of an old church, and in the second, they imply the building of a new one. The first is, probably, nearest to the truth.

[i] His super Antistes (sc. Athelwold), sacro spiramine plenus
   Adhibuit Domino plurima vota suo
Nam fundamen ovans à cardine jecit eoi
   Porticus ut staret ædificata Deo.
Erexitque novum jacto fundamine templum
   Ne tamen expleret raptus ab orbe fuit.

     .   .   .

Vestra cui statim successit in arce potestas
   Et cœptum vigili pectore struxit opus
Insuper occultas studuistis et addere criptas
   Quas sic dedaleum struxerat ingenium
Quisquis ut ignotus veniens intraverat illas
   Nesciat unde meat, quovè pedem referat.
Sunt quibus occultæ latitant quæ hinc inde latebræ
   Quarum tecta patent, intus et antra latent
Introitus quarum stat apertus et exitus harum
   Quas homo qui ignorat luce carere putat
Nocte sub obscurâ quæ stare videntur et umbræ
   Sed tamen occulti lumina solis habent.

     .   .   .

Machina stet quarum, sacram subportat et aram
   Sanctorum pias ordine reliquias
Multiplicique modo manet utile culmen earum
   Exteriora gerens, interiora tegens.
Talia et auxistis hîc Organa, qualia nusquam
   Cernuntur, ...

Thirty lines are now given to a most curious description of the organs, which, however, not being to our present purpose, I shall pass over[k].

[l]" Moreover you have added a lofty temple, in which continual day remains, without night," (to wit,) "a sparkling tower that reflects from heaven the first rays of the rising sun. It has five compartments pierced by open windows, and on all four sides as many ways are open. The lofty peaks of the tower are capped with pointed roofs, and are adorned with various and sinuous vaults, curved with well-skilled contrivance." " Above these stands a rod with golden balls, and at the top a mighty golden cock which boldly turns its face to every wind that blows."

No less than twenty-six lines are bestowed upon the conceits that this last contrivance suggests, and then we come to another dedication at which eight bishops, including Elphegus himself, were present[m]. The king, however, is not mentioned.

[k] See "Essai sur les Instruments de Musique au Moyen Age," by Cousse- maker, in the *Annales Archéologiques*, tom. iv. p. 25, tom. iii. p. 281.

[l] Insuper excelsum fecistis et addere templum
Quo sine nocte manet continuata dies
Turris ab axe micat, quo sol oriendo coruscat
Et spargit lucis spicula prima suæ.
Quinque tenet patulis segmenta oculata fenestris
Per quadrasque plagas pandit ubique vias
Stant excelsa tholis rostrata cacumina turris
Fornicibus variis et sinuata micant.
Quæ sic ingenium docuit curvare perituum
Quod solet in pulcris addere pulcra locis
Stat super auratis virgæ fabricatio bullis
Aureus et totum splendor adornat opus.

Additur ad specimen stat ei quod vertice gallus
Aureus ornatu grandis et intuitu

Impiger imbriferos qui suscipit undique ventos
Seque rotando suam præbet eis faciem.

[m] In describing the two dedications of the church Wolstan enumerates the names of the bishops, but does not mention their sees. It is no small confirmation of his accuracy that they may be nearly all identified. The bishops who attended the first dedication in the time of Ethelwold were, (1.) Dunstan, (2.) Athelwold, (3.) Ælfstan, (4.) Ælfstan, (5.) Æthelgar, (6.) Æscwig, (7.) Ælfheah, (8.) Æthelsin, (9.) Adulfus, (10.) Poca. Those who were present at the second dedication were (11.) Sigericus, (12.) Ælfstan, (13.) Ælfstan, (14.) Ælfheab, (15.) Ordbirht, (16.) Vulfsin, (17.) Ælfric, (18.) Elphegus.

The kindness of John M. Kemble, Esq. has furnished me with the following comments upon these lists. In the year 980, when the first dedication took place, the several sees in England were filled as shewn in the first column of the table below. There is no room therefore for (10.) Poca, and one of three suppositions only is possible; (1.) that he was a chorepiscopus to some other bishop, (2.) that the name is a nickname for some other; Poca, i.e. Pitted with the small pox, (3.) that he was the Cornish bishop either really succeeding Wulfsige, whose name vanishes from my list in 980, or administering as chorepiscopus for him. From the list of bishops given as present at the second dedication, it may be inferred that it took place between the years 993 and 995, in the first of which years Wulfsige became bishop of Sherborne, and in the last of which Sigeric died. Indeed but for a slight uncertainty about Ælfstan of Rochester, who may have lived over 993, one would conclude that the dedication took place in

The church was dedicated to SS. Peter and Paul, as especial patrons. The remainder of the poem is principally devoted to the merits of the saints whose relics are there preserved, and similar topics[n].

that year. The three latter columns of the table contain all the bishops that were living in the years 993, 994, 995. The death of Ælfstan, and consecration of Godwine, are not quite certain.

	980.	993.	994.	995.
Cantuar.	Dunstan (1)	Sigeric (11)	Sigeric	Sigeric
Licetf.	Ælfheah (7)	Ælfheah (14)	Ælfheah	Ælfheah
Legorac.	Æscwig (6)	Æscwig	Æscwig	Æscwig
Wigorn.	Oswald	Ealdwulf	Ealdwulf	Ealdwulf
Hereford	Aðulf	Aðulf	Aðulf	Aðulf
Elmham.	Ðeodred	Ðeodred	Ðeodred	? vac.
Scireburn.	Æðelsige (8)	Wulfsige (16)	Wulfsige	Wulfsige
Winton.	Æðelwold (2)	Ælfheah (18)	Ælfheah	Ælfheah
Selesiens.	Æðelgar (5)	Ordbriht (15)	Ordbriht	Ordbriht
Londin.	Ælfstan (3)	Ælfstan (13)	Ælfstan	Ælfstan
Roffens.	Ælfstan (4)	Ælfstan (12)	? vac.	Godwine
Cridiat.	Ælfric	Ælfwold	Ælfwold	Ælfwold
Ramsbur.	Ælfstan	Ælfric (17)	Ælfric	Ælfric
Fontan.	Sigegar	Sigegar	Sigegar	Sigegar
Eborac.	Oswald	. . . vac. . . .	. . . vac. . . .	Ealdwulf
Lindisf.	Ælfsige	Aldwine	Aldwine	Aldwine
Cornub.	Wulfsige	Ealdred	Ealdred	Ealdred

The list given by John of Exeter (see note c to art. 14) is apparently erroneous, but was probably taken from better authorities. The following prelates may be meant: (1.) *Sigegar. Fontan:* for Sigeric bishop of Ramsbury was not elected till after Æthelwold's death. (2.) *Ælfstan. Lond. Roff. or Ramsb.* all three being alive together. (3.) *Ælfheah Licetf.* (4.) *Ordbriht. Seles.* If not Ordbriht there is no other possible. No such name occurs for several years before or after. But if Ordbriht, then a total blunder, for Ordbriht was not elected till 990, after Dunstan's death. (5.) *Wulfsige Cornub.* (6.) *Ælfric. Crediat.*

[n] From this description it appears that Athelwold rebuilt the monastery as well as the church, and that he was prevented by death from finishing the latter. The crypts were apparently planned, but not executed, during his life, and the line which Milner quotes from Wolstan, and everybody copies from Milner, to prove that Athelwold built the crypts, " Insuper occultas studuistis et addere cryptas," really proves the reverse, and at the same time I am afraid it proves that none of these writers have taken the trouble to go through Wolstan's poem. As the altar stood in the usual manner upon the pavement that surmounted the crypt, it seems that the first dedication of the church took place before even this altar was located, unless indeed we suppose that the crypt was altogether a change of plan after the dedication. When the church was completed, it was dedicated over again. From the description (or rather allusion to) the courts (atria) which the stranger had to pass before he could enter, we learn that there must have been a court of entrance, or western cloister, like those of the well-known early Christian basilicas. It seems too that there were chapels disposed even about this court, of which we have an example in the ancient plan of the monastery of St. Gall. In the church which existed before this of Athelwold, the description of the tomb of Swithun implies that a tower gateway stood before the western entrance, and that the tomb was placed in a similar court in the open air, so that all who entered the church should trample over it. The church had north and south aisles, an eastern apse, and the crypt was probably confined to that apse, as usual in buildings of that age. There were chapels in abundance, to judge from the poem, as well as from the anecdote in (13). The tower which Elphege added stood on four open arches, had five stories with open windows, spiral

18. It appears that Winchester happily escaped the ravages of the Danes at the end of the tenth century. King Canute was a great benefactor to this church, as to many others, and it is said that after the well-known reproof to his courtiers on the sea shore at Southampton, he declined to wear his crown in future, and actually placed it on the head of the crucified image which stood before the high altar of the cathedral of Winchester[o]. He gave also lands called Hille, a large *fere-trum* for the relics of St. Birinus, a silver candelabrum with six branches, such as are now counted most valuable when only made of brass, and two bells[p]. He was buried in the old monastery at Wynton in regal fashion (A.D. 1035). Alwyn, bishop of Winchester, died in 1047, and was first buried in the crypt on the south side of the high altar, but is now (says John of Exeter) placed in a leaden sarcophagus above the door of that crypt on the left hand[q]. Bishop Stigand, out of the gifts of Queen Emma, constructed a great cross with two images of Mary and John, which he gave to Winchester church, together with a beam amply covered with gold and silver. It was placed in the rood-loft (pulpitum). He was buried in the year 1069 at Winchester, in a leaden sarcophagus, on the south side of the high altar[r].

---

staircase vaults, and at each angle, as I understand the description, there was a pointed pinnacle, with balls, a common decoration in ancient drawings. The mighty weathercock surmounts the whole. But like all descriptions of buildings this is very obscure, and its obscurity is increased by the poetical form. After all it admits of being read in various ways, and can only be understood by comparison with cotemporary descriptions and buildings. As most of the early bishops are said to have been buried in the crypt, it does not appear certain that Athelwold gave crypts for the first time to this church.

The line in Wolstan which tells us that Elphege added the crypts to Athelwold's church, seems to have been understood by late writers to mean that Athelwold added crypts to a church that never had them before.

[o] " Rex quoque deinceps Cnuto nunquam coronam portavit sed coronam suam super caput imaginis crucifixi quæ stat in fronte summi altaris in ecclesiâ cathedrali Wyntoniæ, componens, magnum regibus futuris præbuit humilitatis exemplum ut scribit auctor in Concordantiis Historiarum sub literâ K;" Rudborne, 233. "Apud Wyntoniam in veteri monasterio sepelitur more regio." Rudb., 235.

[p] " Anno MXXXV rex Canutus dedit Wintoniensi ecclesiæ terram trium hidarum quæ vocatur Hille et feretrum ad reliquias S. Birini magnum et magni et candelabrum argenteum cum vi brachiis, qualia modò in ecclesiis videmus pretiosissima de aurichalco, et II signa; et in eadem ecclesiâ sepultus est."—Annales, Ecc. Wint., 290.

[q] " Alwynus . . . sepultus fuit primitus in cripta ex parte australi summi altaris, modo vero ponitur in sarcofago plumbeo super ostium illius cripte ex parte sinistra."—John of Exeter, f. 4. 6.

[r] " Stigandus qui magnam crucem ex argento cum ymaginibus argenteis in pulpito ecclesie contulit, sedit annis xxx et jacet in sarcofago plumbeo ex australi parte summi altaris juxta cathedram episcopalem." (John of Exeter, f. 5.) (Ang. Sac., tom. i. p. 285.) "Stigandus . . . de donis Emmæ reginæ condidit magnam crucem cum duabus imaginibus, sc. Mariæ et Johannis; et illas cum trabe vestita auro et argento copiosè dedit Wintoniensi ecclesiæ." Annales, 293. Rudborne seems to refer to the same cross when he says, on

19. Walkelin, the first bishop of Winchester after the Norman Conquest, was appointed to that see in the year 1070. He was a Norman by birth, and related to the Conqueror. His brother Simeon was first made prior of Winchester and then abbot of Ely (A.D. 1082)[s].

In the year 1079, Bishop Walkelin began to rebuild the church of Winton from the foundations[t]; and (in 1086) the king was induced to grant him, for the completion of the church which he had begun, as much wood from the forest of Hanepinges[u] as his carpenters could take in four days and nights. But the bishop collected an innumerable troop of carpenters, and within the assigned time cut down the whole wood, and carried it off to Winchester. Presently after, the king passing by Hanepinges, was struck with amazement, and cried out, Am I bewitched? or have I taken leave of my senses? Had I not once a most delectable wood in this spot? But when he understood the truth, he was violently enraged. Then the bishop put on a shabby vestment, and made his way to the king's feet, humbly begging to resign the episcopate, and merely requesting that he might retain his royal friendship and chaplaincy. And the king was appeased, only observing, "I was as much too liberal in my grant as you were too greedy in availing yourself of it."

20. In the year 1093, in the presence of nearly all the bishops and abbots of England, the monks removed from the old church (*monasterium*) of Winchester to the new one, with great rejoicing and glory, on the sixth idus of April[x] (April 8). And on the feast of Swithun (July 15) they made a procession from the new church to the old, and brought thence the *feretrum* of St. Swithun, which they placed with all honour in the new church. And on the following day the bishop's men first began to pull down the old church, and it was all pulled down in that year except one apse (porticus) and the great

---

the authority of the author " de Concordantiis," that King William gave to the church of Winton, for the soul of Stigand, a great silver cross with two images, which he had found in the bishop's treasury after his death, and that this was all he gave them out of the treasures he found there. (p. 250.)

[s] Annales, Ecc. Wint., p. 294. Rudborne, pp. 255, 256.

[t] "Anno MLXXIX Walkelinus episcopus à fundamentis Wintoniensem cœpit re-ædificare ecclesiam." (Annales, p. 294.)

[u] "Fertur regem concessisse episcopo Walkelino ad perficiendam ecclesiam quam inchoaverat Wintoniensem tantum lignorum de Hanepinges, &c. . . . ."—Annales, p. 295. This is now called Hempage wood, three miles from the city on the road to Alresford. (Milner, 194.)

[x] Probably chosen because it was the day of St. Duvianus, who baptized King Lucius.

altar[y].   In the next year, 1094, relics of St. Swithun and of
many other saints were found under the altar of the old
church[z].

21. The venerable Walkelin, of pious memory, died in the
year 1098.   He greatly improved the church of Winton in
devotion, in the number of its monks, and in the buildings of
the house[a].   He caused the tower of Winton church to be
made as it is still to be seen[b], and rebuilt it, with its four
columns, from the foundations in the middle of the choir[c].
His venerable body is buried in the nave of the church, before
the steps under the rood-loft (pulpitum), in which stands the
silver cross of Stigand, with the two great silver images; and
he lies at the feet of William Gyffard, bishop of Winchester,
having over him a marble stone, with these verses engraved
thereon :

> " Præsul Walklynus istic requiescit humatus
> Tempore Willelmi Conquestoris cathedratus[d]."

22. When King William Rufus was slain by the arrow of
Walter Tirrel in the New Forest, (A.D. 1100,) his body was
brought to Winchester, and buried in the cathedral church,
in the middle of the choir[e].   It was laid in the ground within
the limits of the tower, in the presence of many nobles, but
with the tears of few.   Some years afterwards (namely, in
the year 1107[f]) the tower fell, which many thought to have
been a judgment for his sins; and because that it was a

[y] "Anno mxciij. In præsentiâ omnium
ferè episcoporum atque abbatum Angliæ
cum maximâ exultatione et gloriâ de veteri monasterio Wintoniensi ad novum
venerunt monachi VI. idus Aprilis. Ad
festum verò S. Swithuni factâ processione
de novo monasterio ad vetus, tulerunt inde
feretrum S. Swithuni et in novo honorificè
collocaverunt. Sequenti die verò Domini
Walkelini episcopi cœperunt homines primum vetus frangere monasterium; et frac-
tum est totum in illo anno, excepto por-
ticu uno et magno altari." Annales, p. 295.

[z] "Anno mxciv . . . . . . inventæ sunt
reliquiæ S. Swithuni aliorumque plurimo-
rum sanctorem sub altari veteris monasterii." Annales, p. 295.

[a] " . . . . Ecclesiam Wintoniensem in
religione et numero monachorum et in domorum ædificiis plurimum melioravit."
Annales, p. 296.

[b] Walkelinus episcopus fieri fecit turrim ecclesiæ Wyntoniensis ut modo cernitur." Rudborne, p. 256.

[c] " Walkelinus nacione Normannus qui
turrim in medio chori cum quatuor co-
lumpnis a fundamentis renovavit seditque
xxix annis et in navi ecclesie ante gradus
pulpiti jacet humatus." (John of Exeter,
f. 5.) (Ang. Sacr., tom. i. p. 285.)

[d] Jacet enim ejusdem præsulis venera-
bile corpus humatum in navi ecclesiæ ad
gradus sub pulpito in quo erigitur crux ar-
gentea magna Stigandi archiepiscopi cum
duabus imaginibus argenteis magnis, ad
pedes viz. Willelmi Gyffard quondam Wyntoniensi episcopi; et in lapide marmoreo
superposito sculpuntur hi versus; Præsul,
&c. . . ." (Rudborne, p. 256.)

[e] "Tandem Wyntoniæ deportatur et in
ecclesiâ cathedrali sepelitur in medio chori
hæc Matthæus Parisiacensis de morte regis Willelmi Rufi." Rudborne, p. 270.
In the printed copy of Matt. Par., however, I find no mention of the choir.

[f] "Anno MCVII. Turris ecclesiæ cecidit Nonis Octobris." Ann. Wint., p. 297.

grievous wrong to bury in that sacred place one who ·all his life had been profane and sensual, and who died without the Christian viaticum—thus Rudborne. Malmesbury cautiously declines to give an opinion upon this matter, because, as he says, it may have been after all that the structure would have fallen from the instability of its workmanship, whether the body had been buried there or not[g].

23. " But now (says Rudborne) an apparent contradiction arises, for it is written in the archives of the church of Wynton, that Bishop Walkelin built the tower in question. But he died in the eleventh year of King Rufus, (about two years before that monarch ;) and the tower does not appear to have fallen after it was erected by Walkelin ; it is of the strongest construction, and is to this day, in the opinion of masons, the very firmest of this kind of tower in all England. The answer to this is, that the truth of those who say that the tower fell for the sins of Rufus, is thus to be explained. That Walkelyn did not build the tower during his life, but that after his death the old tower of the church having fallen after the king was buried within it, it was rebuilt out of the great funds which Walkelyn left to this church. And that as it was built with his money, although after his death, yet his name was associated with it as the founder. This is the opinion of the author of the Concordance of English History, under the letter V,

[g] " Pauci rusticanorum cadaver in rheda caballaria compositum Wintoniam in episcopatum devexere, cruore undatim per totam viam stillante. Ibi infra ambitum turris multorum procerum conventu paucorum planctu terræ traditum. Secuta est posteriora anno ruina turris, de qua re, quæ opiniones fuerint, parco dicere, ne videar nudis nugis magis credere ; præsertim cum pro instabilitate operis machina ruinam fecisse potuisset, etiamsi ipse nunquam ibi sepultus fuisset." Will. Malms., p. 126.

" Neque defuêre opiniones quorundam dicentium, ruinam turris quæ posterioribus annis accidit, peccatis illius contigisse ; quod injuria fuerit illum sancto tumulari loco, qui tota vitâ petulans et lubricus, moriens etiam Christiano caruerit viatico. Sed videtur quòd hîc contrarietus possit oriri ; ut enim habetur in scriptis Wyntoniensi ecclesiæ, Walkelinus episcopus Wyntoniæ turrim illam fabricavit, qui anno undecimo Wilhelmi regis Rufi obiit, et non invenitur post illam fabricationem quæ facta est per Walkelinum, turrim illam cecidisse ; quia fortissima turris

facta est et adhuc extat secundum latomos firmissima inter omnes hujusmodi turres in regno Angliæ. Ad istud respondendum est ; quod veritas taliter opinantium, quòd pro peccatis Wilhelmi regis Rufi eo ibidem sepulto turris ipsa cecidit, habetur isto modo, Walkelynus ejusdem sedis episcopus in vitâ suâ turrim ipsam non fecit fieri, sed post ipsius mortem antiquâ turri ipsius ecclesiæ, sepulto in eâ Wilhelmo rege Rufo, cadente, de maximâ quantitate sive summâ pecuniæ quam Walkelynus præsul suæ ecclesiæ legavit in suo decessu ad ejusdem ecclesiæ necessaria providenda, sufficiens portio sumpta est pro sumptibus ad novam turrim fabricandam. Et .quia de bonis ipsius Walkelyni fabricata est quamvis post mortem ejus ; tamen nomen fundatoris ipsius turris, sicut dignum est, sibi retinet ; quæ turris usque hodie firmissima stat. Istud est dictum auctoris de Concordantiis Historiarum Angliæ sub litera V. Ipse enim auctor multa scribit de ecclesiâ Wyntoniensi in qua quondam nutritus erat." Rudborne, p. 271.

who wrote much concerning the church of Winchester, in which he had been educated." I shall discuss this opinion in the next chapter, after describing the present state of the tower and adjacent parts of the church.

24. In the year 1111 the relics of St. Athelwold were taken from the old feretrum and placed in a new one, in presence of the queen, and of three bishops, and five abbots[h]. And in 1150 the relics of the holy confessors Birinus, Swithun, Edda, Birstan, and Elfege, were translated[i].

But in the time of Henry de Blois, who held this see from 1129 to 1171, there appears from the several passages that follow to have been a general translation of the bodies of the old kings and bishops, probably from the site of the old Saxon crypt. "The Christian kings of the West Saxons buried in the church of Wynton were Kyngils, Kynewald his son, who completed the work of the church which his father began, and was buried ˌunder (or before) the high altar, Estuin, Kentwyn, Athellard, brother of Queen Fretheswythe, and Kenulph, whose bodies were buried together in the eastern crypt, as Vigilantius recordeth in his ' Basilica Petri.' Afterwards, in the days of Henry of Blois, these were translated, but not knowing which were kings and which were bishops, because there were no inscriptions over the monuments, the aforesaid Henry placed in leaden sarcofagi kings and bishops, bishops and kings, all mixed together, as it is recorded in the book of the acts of Bishops William and Henry, by Robert, prior of Winton[k]."

[h] "Anno MCXI .... depositæ sunt Reliquiæ S. Adelwoldi de veteri feretro et impositæ in novo. Interfuit autem regina et tres episcopi et quinque abbates." Ann. Wint. 297.

[i] "Anno MCL translatæ sunt Reliquiæ Sanctorum Confessorum Birini, Swithuni, Æddæ, Bristani, Elphegi." Ann. Wint. 300.

[k] John of Exeter, from whom I have copied the above, also gives the names of the Saxon pagan kings who were buried in the church, when it was a temple of Dagon; but with considerable poetry of imagination he represents their bones to have been consumed by the burning words of Birinus, when he consecrated the church. I have inserted the whole passage below.

"Ex regno Westsaxonum quod Gewyseorum dicitur plurimi reges ac in armis principes strenui processerunt de quorum numero quinque reges pagani dummodo templum esset Dagon quod modo dicitur vetus cœnobium consepulti sunt, Cerdicius, Cenricius, Cedulinus, Celricius, Ceowlphus; qui omnes ut scribit Gerardus Cornubiensis de gestis regum Westsaxonum *cap. sexto.* Dum beatus Birinus primus Anglie et Gewyseorum apostolus, ministeria dedicationis ecclesie Wentane rite perageret subito voces lamentantium gementiumque audite sunt clamantes, Ve nobis, Ve nobis, Ve nobis, quod prodest esse princeps ac dominus orbis et in inferno ad ultimum sine fine concremari. Ecce verba sancti Birini ossa nostra incendunt et in pulverem redigunt ; superque hiis locis sepulchrorum perscrutatis nulla vestigia sepultorum visa sunt. Corpora vero Christianorum regum Westsaxonum ante monarchiam sepulta in Wentana ecclesia hec sunt, Kyngilsus qui Chylcombe dedit, Kynewaldus filius Kyngilsi qui opus ecclesie ҁ patre inceptum complevit et tria maneria

"Matilda queen of England, commonly called Molde the good Queen, died in 1118, and was buried at Winchester in the old monastery, where this epitaph is to be seen on a marble stone over the place of her burial in the eastern crypt. ' Here lieth Matilda the Queen, daughter of Margaret Queen of Scotland, and wife of King Henry the First, called by the English Molde the good Queen.' Nevertheless, in certain other monasteries of England a tomb may be seen to her as if she were buried there, although her true place of sepulture is in the old monastery of Winton. Her bones, however, were translated by Henry of Blois, and placed in a leaden sarcophagus, together with those of the noble Queen Frytheswyda, the mother of St. Frytheswyda, over the place which is called *The Holy Hole.*" Moreover, "Edmund, the first-born of King Alfred, was buried in the old monastery of Wynton, as appears from the marble stone of his tomb, which lies still on the north of the altar where matutinal or capitular mass is celebrated. And the epitaph written thereon is *Here lieth Edmund the King, son of King Aldred.* But his bones are now translated to a certain sarcophagus placed over the *Holy Hole,* as it is written in the book of the acts of the Bishops William and Henry[1]."

eidem ecclesie dedit, viz., Donnton Alresford et Wordiam qui sepultus est sub summo altari. Estuini, Kentwyni, Athellardique fratris Fretheswythe regine, Kenulphi, quorum corpora consepulta erant in orientali cripta ut scribit Vigilantius de bas[a]. Petri, c. vi. sed postmodum tempore Henrici Blesensi translata sunt et propter ignoranciam qui essent reges et qui essent episcopi et quod non erant tituli inscripti supra monumenta eorum predictus Henricus posuit in sarcofagis plumbeis reges cum episcopis et episcopos cum regibus sic permixtos ut habetur in quodam libello Roberti prioris Wintoniensis et postmodum Glastoniensis abbatis de actibus Willelmi et Henrici episcoporum." (John of Exeter, f. 5. b.) Rudborne, p. 194, has also quoted the last passage concerning Henry of Blois.

[1] "A⁰. D[i]. MCXVIII. et anno regni Regis Henrici primi nono decimo obiit Matildis Regina Anglie. Anglice usque in hodiernum diem appellata 𝕱𝖑𝖔𝖑𝖉𝖊 𝖙𝖍𝖊 𝖌𝖔𝖔𝖉 𝕼𝖚𝖊𝖓𝖊; et secundum auctorem in Flores Historiarum Wyntoniæ in Veteri Monasterio sepulta est et idem habetur in scriptis ejusdem monasterii. Nam habetur consimile epitaphium ejusdam in quo-

dam lapide marmoreo posito super locum sepulturæ ipsius Reginæ in cryptâ orientali *Hic jacet Matildis Regina filia Margaretæ Reginæ Scotiæ et uxor Regis Henrici primi, ab Anglis vocata,* 𝕱𝖔𝖑𝖉𝖊 𝖙𝖍𝖊 𝖌𝖔𝖔𝖉 𝕼𝖚𝖊𝖓. Attamen in quibusdam monasteriis Angliæ fit tumba ipsius, ac si ibidem jaceret; sed in rei veritate sepulturæ locum habuit in prædicto Veteri Cenobio Wyntoniæ. Cujus sanctissimæ regina ossa modo per Henricum Blesensem et fratrem Regis Stephani ac nepotem hujus Regis Henrici primi ex sorore Adalâ translata sunt, et posita in sarcophago plumbeo cum ossibus nobilissimæ Frytheswydæ reginæ matris sanctæ Frytheswydæ virginis supra locum vocatum, 𝕿𝖍𝖊 𝕳𝖔𝖑𝖞 𝕳𝖔𝖑𝖊." (Rudborne, p. 276.) "(Edmundus filius primogenitus Alfredi regis) . . . . . . in veteri monasterio Wyntoniensi sepelitur; ut satis clarè patet intuentibus lapidem marmoreum tumbæ ipsius qui jacet adhuc in terrâ ex boreali parte altaris ubi missa matutinalis sive capitularis celebratur. Et est epitaphium in marmore scriptum istud ; *Hic jacet Edmundus Rex filius Aldredi Regis* . . . . . . Ossa vero Edmundi regis jam translata sunt in quoddam sarcophagum locatum super locum nuncupatum 𝕿𝖍𝖊 𝕳𝖔𝖑𝖞 𝕳𝖔𝖑𝖊:

CHAPTER II.

ON THE CRYPTS AND TRANSEPTS.

HAVING in the last chapter brought down the history of the building to the end of the twelfth century, it is time to compare it with the building itself. The present cathedral is in the form of a cross. The transepts, of a rude and plain Norman, manifest themselves at first sight as the oldest part of the edifice. A central tower, also Norman, stands upon four piers of great and unusual magnitude, and of singularly close jointed masonry. A superficial examination is sufficient to shew that this tower is of subsequent workmanship to the transepts. The eastern arm of the cross is of a mixed work, including portions of Early English, Decorated, and Perpendicular; the eastern extremity is bounded by a high gable, and beyond this is a low Early English structure, which consists of three aisles of nearly equal height, each of which terminates eastward in a chapel. The central one of these chapels, known as the Lady-chapel, is Early English in its western compartment, but has received an elongation of Perpendicular work, which is the most easterly part of the whole church. Beneath the eastern arm of the cross are crypts of the same rude Norman work as the transepts. They (like many others) serve to shew us the original plan of the Norman church, and it thus appears that its presbytery was terminated eastward by a round apse, at the point where now the flat Perpendicular gable stands.

The aisles of the Norman presbytery were continued round this apse, and a small round-ended (Lady-?)chapel extended as far as the western arch of the present one; also two small eastern towers flanked the apse of the presbytery. A crypt seems to have been also erected under the Early English Lady-chapel, but the crypt of the Perpendicular addition to this chapel is extended westward, and thus occupies a greater space in that direction than the Perpendicular compartment above it, by which means its vault intrudes upon and cuts off the original Early English vault, the remains of which, denuded

ut invenitur in quodam Libello Roberti quondam hujus ecclesiæ præpositi postmodum abbatis Westmonasterii de *gestis* *Wilhelmi et Henrici Pontificum.*" (Rudborne, p. 207.)

of ribs, which now lie between the end of the Norman Lady-chapel crypt, and the later Perpendicular crypt, have induced some observers to believe that they had found traces of a very ancient building indeed.

The nave, or western arm of the cross, was originally Norman, and is now early Perpendicular; the transformation from one style to the other, for it was not rebuilt, presents one of the most curious studies imaginable. The present western termination is a flat front, but from foundations that still exist, and have been excavated and examined in the last year, it appears that the Norman cathedral extended about forty feet farther westward, and had enormous western towers. I will now proceed to examine the different parts, thus concisely indicated, in detail.

The general style of the transepts may be understood from

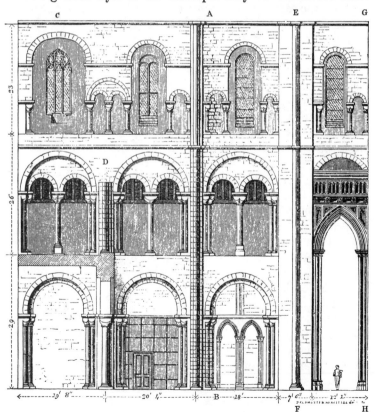

Fig 1   West Elevation of South Transept.

the elevation, fig. 1. This represents the western wall of the south transept. The architecture is of the plainest description. The compartment of the triforium is very nearly of the same height as that of the pier-arches, and the clerestory is also nearly the same height. In this respect the distribution of Winchester resembles that of Ely, Peterborough, and Norwich, and the actual altitude of the walls in the three first examples are very nearly the same, being 75 ft., 72 ft., 76 ft. respectively, but Norwich is only 64 ft. At Winchester each pier-arch is formed of two orders or courses of voussoirs, the edges of which are left square, wholly undecorated by moldings. This is the case with the pier-arches of Ely transept, but in the arches of the triforium of Ely, and in every other Norman part of that cathedral and of the other two above cited, the edges of the voussoirs are richly molded. In Winchester transept, on the contrary, the arches of the triforium and clerestory are square edged like those of the pier-arches below, and hence arises the peculiarly simple and massive effect of this part of the church[m].

These transepts (as at Ely) have both eastern and western aisles. Peterborough has only eastern, and Norwich none at all. But Winchester, in addition, has also at each end of the transept an aisle, which rises only to the pier-arch level, and consists of two arches only, which rest in the middle on a triple bearing-shaft instead of the compound pier, which is employed throughout the rest of the work.

This kind of gallery is not unusual in the churches of Normandy, as I have already had occasion to remark in my History of Canterbury[n], where I have shewn that it was reserved for chapels, or for the preservation of relics of peculiar sanctity. At each end of the platform above the gallery at the level of the triforium, an engaged shaft, with pier edges behind it, springs from the face of the wall, but is carried up only a little above the capitals of the triforium arches, and there terminates abruptly, as at *D* in fig. 1, and at this part of the wall the masonry is disturbed as if something had once projected from the wall and has been removed. Whether there was once an arcade across the front of the gallery, or a beam of the nature of a roodbeam, or what other contrivance, it is impossible now to say. But it is clear that the shaft in

---

[m] Britton, pl. 12, has an excellent perspective view of the north transepts.

[n] Architectural History of Canterbury Cathedral, p. 37, note l.

question could not have been carried up to the roof like its neighbour at *A*, because the clerestory immediately over it has a pair of small open arches so placed as to make such a disposition impossible, as the figure clearly shews.

But the structure of these transepts shews that they were erected at two different periods, and that when the second erection took place changes were also introduced into the previous work. Each transept exactly resembles the other in these respects.

The vaults of the compartments *C D E F G* in the plan°

Fig 2 One Bay of North Transept.

are plain groined vaults. But those of the eastern compartments, *H, I, K*, are ribbed; one of these compartments is shewn in fig. 2. The Decorated window is a manifest insertion of later times. Now the general and original plan of

---

° The general plan of the cathedral will be found at the end of the paper.

the transept piers is that shewn in the darker tint of fig. 3, and the piers *d* and *k* of the general plan remain in this state. But

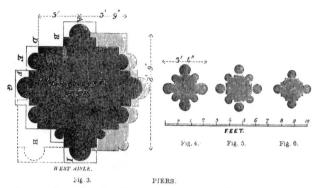

Fig. 4.   Fig. 5.   Fig. 6.

Fig. 3.   PIERS.

the pier *m* has received a subsequent addition to its north-western angle, which changes its form to that represented by the dotted line in fig. 3. Its western face now presents two engaged shafts of equal magnitude with a plain wall between, instead of one only as in the original plan. The evidences of this change are shewn by the joints of the masonry, and by the capital and its abacus, in a way that when once pointed out cannot be mistaken. Also the half-pier on the opposite west wall has been similarly augmented, and the arch which rests upon these piers has been more than doubled in breadth. Fig. 7. is a view of this arch and altered pier as seen by a spectator standing in the compartment *F*, with his back against the north wall.

In this view the original engaged shaft has a ring round it, the added shaft (nearest to the spectator) is plain; the piecing of the abacus is shewn, and the original capital of the small vaulting-shaft is seen peeping out between the two. That the vault of this compartment was

Fig. 7. North west Corner of N. Transept

erected before this change is plain, because it passes through and behind the new arch, as the figure shews, and the new pier also blocks up part of the arcade which decorates the wall below the window, and is crowded awkwardly against the window.

Now, in the compartment *H*, the same kind of addition has been made to the transept pier *n* and to the half pier of the wall *p*, and this half pier obstructs the window-arch of the eastern wall. But the vault of this compartment is ribbed, as before stated, and these ribs, instead of passing behind the additional part of the pier, are made to abut upon it in a way that clearly shews this ribbed vault to have been erected in connexion with, or at least subsequently to, the change. From this I infer, that the plain groined vaults are of the original structure, and that the additions to the piers, together with the ribbed vaults, belong to the second structure.

The motive for this additional strength given to the arches and piers at *o, p*, will appear if we examine the outside of the building. There, from many symptoms, it is shewn that square towers were to have been erected on the compartments *E* and *H*, to flank the gable of the transept. Fig. 8. is a sketch of part of the north-east corner of the north transept. This shews an unfinished turret at the corner, the springing of an arcade above, with other marks that shew that the north wall of the side aisle was to have been carried up vertically as for the side of a tower. Moreover, the northernmost clerestory window is inserted under an arch which was meant to open into the tower.

Fig. 8.   North-east Corner of N. Transept.

Whether the tower ever existed and has been removed, or whether it was only projected and prepared for, I cannot tell. But traces of similar towers may be found more or less distinct at each angle of the transepts, namely, two towers

flanking the north gable, and two the south.   In the interior
elevation of the transept (fig. 1.) the clerestory window at *C* is
placed under a wider arch than the other.   This is one of the
arches which were to have opened into the tower.   I should
have stated that the nature and colour of the masonry outside
shews two periods, the first of which terminates just below
the billet-molded tablet in fig. 8, and therefore includes the
pier-arches alone.

I conclude from all these appearances that the transepts
were begun without towers, and that after they had risen to
the height of the pier-arches the work was interrupted : when
it was resumed, the towers formed a part of the new plan, and
it became necessary to fortify the arches of the previous work
to enable them to carry them.   It must be observed that the
eastern arch of the compartment *E* (in the general plan) is in
its original form a strong arch, because it has to carry the
entire height of the transept wall up to the clerestory.   Therefore it needed no additional strength.   But the southern arch
of this compartment in the original plan was merely a transverse rib separating the vaults, and having no wall above it.
This made it necessary to strengthen it when the tower was
planned.

I must now explain another singular addition or change in
the original plan.   The portions of the transepts which I have
just described, namely, the extreme northern and southern
parts of the cross, are of rough masonry and workmanship,
but not greater than that of early Norman work in general.
But the four piers of the central tower, as well as the two
piers contiguous to them in each transept, although of Norman work, are of singularly good masonry, and their form is
more square and stronger than those of the other transept
piers.   These eight piers are distinguished from the others in
the plan by a different tint.

The arches also which are in connexion with these piers are
of the same close-jointed masonry; and there can be no doubt
that all this portion of the work has been rebuilt; thus con-
firming the account which history has given us, that the tower
fell after the burial of William Rufus, and was rebuilt.
Fig. 1. shews more clearly the line of demarcation between
the two kinds of masonry, and therefore the exact portions
that were rebuilt.   The pier *A B* is of the older work; *E F* of
the newer work;   *G H* is the tower-pier.

The arches of the clerestory, triforium, and lower range, between EF and AB, are all of the newer masonry, while the shafts that project from AB, and upon which these arches rest, are of the older style. This would necessarily be the case, for if the pier EF were rebuilt, the arches that rested upon it must also have been rebuilt. But the plan of the new pier is different from the others, and as we may suppose that the pier which occupied its place before the fall of the tower was like its neighbouring pier in the transept, we are led to the conclusion that the plan of the new pier differs from that of the old. The elevation EF shews that this new pier is broader and simpler than the old one AB. But the change of form is shewn more distinctly in fig. 3. The dark shade is the old transept pier; the light shade on the right hand is the additional portion, or a plan of half the newer transept pier in question[p]. It will be observed, that the pier in its new form is considerably stronger than before, although the same number of shafts are disposed upon the respective faces; that, in fact, the general arrangement of the parts of the old pier form a circular group, or rather a square, with the angles turned to the aisle; but that in the new form the parts group into a square, with its side turned to the aisle. The transverse measurement of the new pier is the same as before, but the longitudinal measure (that parallel to the aisles) is somewhat increased, and as the whole mass of the pier is moved nearer to the tower, the arches between AB and EF, fig. 1, retain nearly the same span as before, but the arches between EF and GH are very considerably narrowed.

The tower-piers themselves must have undergone a considerable increase of dimensions. They are at present most unwieldy and intrusive, from their excessive size and awkward squareness of form, and are the largest tower-piers in England in proportion to the spans of the arches that rest on them.

Fig. 9. (see next page) is a plan of the south-western pier, upon the same scale as the plans of the other piers. I have drawn upon this, in a darker tint, the plan that, in all probability, was that of the former pier which fell.

It will be seen that the newer pier is of a square and simple form, very unusual in Norman piers.

[p] The dotted line on the left of this plan has already been explained to mean the addition to the extreme pier, and does not concern the present question.

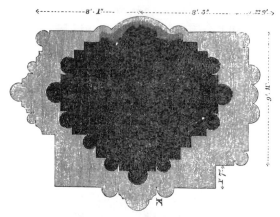

Fig. 9   South-western Tower Pier.

Figure 10. represents, upon the same scale, the south-

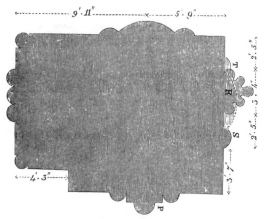

Fig. 10.   South-eastern Pier.

eastern pier, which, with some difference, is like the last.   It
may be worth while to remark the excessive change in the
dimensions of piers that took place during the successive ages
in which the present church was completed.

In figs. 3, 4, and 5, the transept pier is shewn in comparison
with the piers of the choir and its eastern aisles; and it must
be remembered, that the walls carried by them all are of the
same altitude, but that increased mechanical experience had
taught the builders to reduce both the thickness of their walls,
and the size and number of their piers.   In fig. 10. *R*
shews the half pier or respond of the choir-arch, (namely, half

of fig. 4.) *TS* are the remaining fragments which may be seen of the original Norman respond, which occupies more than twice the space. The piers however present a greater contrast of magnitude than the walls they support, for the Norman wall is of the same thickness as its pier; but the Decorated wall of the choir is considerably thicker than the pier which it overhangs on each side. The pier is 3 ft. 4 in. diameter, and its wall 5 ft. 5 in., whereas the Norman wall is 6 ft. 2 in., the same as *D H*, fig. 3, namely, that part of the pier upon which it stands.

This sketch, fig. 11, (taken however from the north-eastern pier,) shews the Decorated respond, and the remains of the Norman respond by the side of it[q].

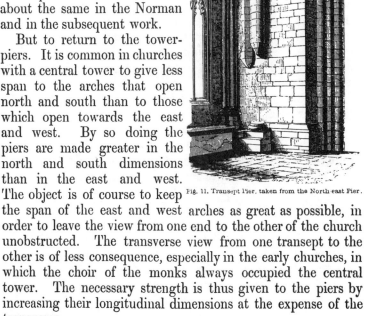

The distance from the centre of one pier to that of the next is about the same in the Norman and in the subsequent work.

But to return to the tower-piers. It is common in churches with a central tower to give less span to the arches that open north and south than to those which open towards the east and west. By so doing the piers are made greater in the north and south dimensions than in the east and west. The object is of course to keep

Fig. 11. Transept Pier, taken from the North east Pier.

the span of the east and west arches as great as possible, in order to leave the view from one end to the other of the church unobstructed. The transverse view from one transept to the other is of less consequence, especially in the early churches, in which the choir of the monks always occupied the central tower. The necessary strength is thus given to the piers by increasing their longitudinal dimensions at the expense of the transverse.

q The base of the Norman respond happens to be on this side more mutilated than the figure shews it, but we took the liberty of supplying this from the southern pier (at *S*, in the general plan.)

This artifice is carried to a much greater excess in some
examples than in others.   In Winchester to the greatest.
But Gloucester and Hereford have very oblong piers.   Peterborough too may be quoted, but is not completely in excess,
although its squareness of form brings it into this class.   In
Norwich, Durham, St. Alban's, and St. Stephen at Caen, the
shafts and pier-edges are managed so as to throw the tower-
pier into the mass of a square, or rather parallelogram, with
its angles turned towards the aisles[r].

This diagonal position is, with very few exceptions, the
general system of the piers in the succeeding periods, and it
gives a free passage for light and for access between the piers.
When the pier is in the square position, it resembles a portion
of wall, and the pier-arch is reduced to a mere arch in that
wall.   But when the diagonal position is employed, the pier,
however compound its arrangement, always resolves itself into
one or more columns, upon which the arches rest, with
greater lightness of effect, and with greater apparent span.   In
the tower of Winchester, from the excess to which the opposite system is carried out, the arches that open from the tower
to the transepts are reduced to narrow arches in a very thick
wall, and the interior of these transepts is quite hidden from
the choir and presbytery, at a very small distance on each side
of the centre of the tower.

There can be no doubt that these piers were erected under
the influence of the panic caused by the fall of the tower,
and that having no certain principles to guide them in determining the necessary dimensions for strength, the builders
contented themselves by making the piers as large as the place
would admit, sacrificing beauty and fitness to necessity.   And
this is really the history of all constructions.   It is a great
mistake to suppose that the architects of old were governed
by scientific principles; practice and experience taught them the
necessary proportions.   They began by making their struc-
tures as strong as they could; if from bad workmanship and
unequal settlements the building fell, they made it so much
the bigger next time.   Finding it now too large they reduced
the next building of the kind, and so on, by gradual experi-
ments, were brought to proportions at once safe and beautiful.
But all their works shew that they had no just conceptions of

---

[r] The ordinary piers of Norwich cathedral, on the other hand, are remarkable examples of the square position.

statical principles, and that they were guided by natural ingenuity alone, assisted by the numerous opportunities which the middle ages afforded for the erection of churches.

There is some difficulty in determining, from the historical documents that have reached us, the exact history of this early portion of the church. In the first chapter it has been shewn that Bishop Athelwold, about the year 980, effected a thorough repair, if not an entire rebuilding, of the church and monastery; that his successor added crypts, or rather, as I understand it, that he made more extensive crypts than had previously existed. And from the excessive praise and florid descriptions which are given to these works by cotemporary writers, so exalted an idea of their magnitude and beauty has been conveyed, that many persons have thought it impossible that in less than a century Walkelin should have thought it necessary to demolish them entirely. Thus Milner imagines that the crypts of the present church are the work of Athelwold, "the walls, pillars, and groining of which remain in much the same state as he left them in[s];" and also that the eastern arm of the cross of the Saxon church was allowed by Walkelin to remain, and was only pulled down when the present presbytery was erected[t]. But, as Mr. Britton has well observed[u], "it is a favourite maxim with some antiquaries to carry back the date of every church as far as possible, and like the late Mr. King and Mr. Carter, they do not hesitate to assert peremptorily that the oldest part must be of the age of the first foundation."

The argument from rudeness of workmanship, is best answered by comparing the transepts of Winchester with Norman buildings erected in places where no Saxon cathedral stood before, and where, therefore, there can be no supposition of the kind above stated. Thus the masonry of these transepts is

Fig. 13.   North Transept.

[s] Milner's Winchester, p. 8. Mr. Garbett, of Winchester, however, (in a letter printed by Britton in his Winchester Cathedral, p. 57,) actually distributes the work of the present cathedral as follows. The western crypt of the lady chapel he gives to King Lucius. The lower part of the transepts to King Kenewalch. The upper part of the transepts, with the greater crypt and the original nave, to Athelwold; and the central tower and parts adjacent to Walkelin.

[t] Milner, vol. i. p. 13.

[u] Britton's Winchester, p. 70.

not more rude in its tooling, and the width of its joints, than that of Norwich cathedral, which see was removed from Thetford after the Conquest. Again, the architecture, in design as well as roughness of workmanship, of Winchester transept, is nearly identical even in dimensions with that of Ely transept, as they would naturally be, as the work of the brothers Walkelin and Simeon.

That many of the Saxon churches were erected of stone, and on plans of great complexity, with crypts, triforia, clerestories, central towers, and other parts resembling in arrangement the Norman churches, can hardly be doubted, from the descriptions that have been preserved to us. But that in dimensions and decoration they at all equalled the churches of their successors is wholly improbable. That cotemporary writers should praise them as immeasurably lofty and spacious is natural, and in perfect accordance with the practice of all writers, who necessarily imagine the great works of their own age to be the greatest works possible, because they have never seen anything better or half so good. Perhaps the best testimony to their comparative merit is given by Bishop Wolstan, of Worcester.

He, after the Conquest, had erected a new church there, to replace the Saxon church which his predecessor Oswald had built (c. 980). It was on a different site, and when the new church was sufficiently advanced to be occupied by the monks, he ordered the old church, the work of the blessed Oswald, to be unroofed and pulled down. But Wolstan, standing in the open air and looking on, could not restrain his tears at the sight, saying, " We wretched people destroy the works of the saints, that we may get praise for ourselves. That age of happy men knew not how to construct pompous edifices, but they knew well how, under such roofs as they had, to sacrifice themselves to God, and to set a good example. We, alas ! strive that we may pile up stones, neglecting the while the cure of souls[x]." Whatever allowance may be made for the Saxon feelings of Wolstan, himself a Saxon bishop amongst Normans, and therefore in all probability unfriendly to the new modes, yet the phraseology necessarily implies a strong and undeniable contrast between the Saxon and Norman practice and manner of building, and an apology for the inferiority of the former.

[x] Malm. de gest. Pont., lib. iv. p. 280.

If Rudborne's history (or John of Exeter's) alone had been preserved to us, we should have been in greater difficulties, for there we find no other work of Walkelin expressly recorded but the tower and its piers. But the account given in the Annals is so clear that we cannot doubt that Walkelin rebuilt the church, or began it at least, and continued it so far that the monks were able to occupy it. It even appears that it was on a different site from the Saxon one, for the choir was ready for service before the old church was begun to be demolished; and although from the phrase that in one year the whole was destroyed save only one apse (or porticus) and the high altar, some have concluded that that apse was retained in the new building, it seems to me that the phrase that follows shews that the work of demolition went on, the old altar was destroyed, and probably with it the rest of the old building. That the position of the two buildings was different appears from the old tomb of Swithun, which the Saxon Wolstan says was on the west side of the church, but in Rudborne's days it was to be seen at the north door. This proves, at least, that the present church is much longer, and perhaps even that the present church stands farther south. This would be true if Wolstan's words be taken exactly to mean that the tomb stood *opposite* the west end. And if we suppose the Saxon cathedral to have had a court in front of the west end, with a tower gateway of entrance, then Swithun's tomb would be exactly in the line of the passengers, so as to be trampled under foot, according to his desire. But it may be that the tomb stood north-west, which might be loosely described as west. As we know that the old high altar was in a different spot from the new one, and that the choir of the new church was built first, and occupied the same space as the present one, as shewn by the crypt, I incline to place the Saxon cathedral across the present north transept, which would thus require it to be pulled down to complete the latter.

The crypt of the present church cannot have been any part of the Saxon church, for the reasons above stated shew that the high altars were on different sites. Indeed the plan of the present crypt is in perfect accordance with that of Norman churches in general, and is of very great extent. The identity of the work of the crypt with that of the transept may be shewn by a peculiar abacus which is used in the crypt, and also in the column which stands at each end of each transept, bearing the gallery already described. Fig. 13. shews one of the capitals in the crypt, and fig. 14. that in the north transept. They are distinguished by an abacus so thin that it deserves the name better than any other example I have seen; and by the unusual combination (in Norman pillars) of a *round* capital with a *square* abacus, as in the Doric order.

That Rufus was buried in the central tower, and not in some other tower, as some have supposed, is plain, because one account says he was buried in the middle of the choir. As therefore the choir, like that of all Norman cathedrals in their original state, stands under the central tower, that must be the place of Rufus' burial. But the tower has plainly been rebuilt, and the account that it fell after Rufus' death, even if its fall had not been recorded in the Annals, is too well authenticated to be denied. Therefore we arrive at the conclusion that Walkelin built a tower on this site, together with the transepts, and that his tower fell after the death of Rufus, and was replaced by the existing one, but I am not sure that the curious discussion which Rudborne has quoted has given us the right conclusion, namely, that the present tower being built with Walkelin's funds, does therefore bear his name, for Walkelin may have been recorded as the builder of the tower that fell. Still it shews that doubts had arisen in the middle ages about the history of this tower. I have shewn that Walkelin's transepts went on slowly, and with changes of plan.

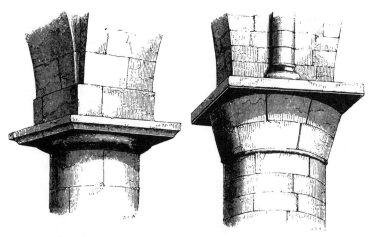

Fig 13. Capital in Crypt.   Fig. 14 Capital of North Transept.

It is worth observing, in comparing Winchester and Ely, the cotemporary works of the brothers Walkelin and Simeon, that they were both erected on different sites from their previous Saxon churches, and moreover that the central towers of both of them fell in after ages, Walkelin's in 1107, and Simeon's in 1321.

CHAPTER III.

ON THE EASTERN PART OF THE CHURCH.

THE eastern arm of the church, in its present state, affords specimens of every style of architecture from the Conquest to the Reformation, and it is greatly to be regretted that so little of its history has reached us, with the exception of the beginning of the work.

Bishop Godfrey de Lucy held the see from 1189 to 1204. In 1200 the Annals record that "the tower of Winchester church was begun and finished[y]." Which tower and what work was so quickly effected does not appear. The upper story of the central tower is wholly decorated with round-headed arches, and, according to all likelihood, is fifty years earlier than this period.

In 1202, "the bishop instituted a confraternity for the reparation of the church of Winton, to last for five complete years." And in the Obituary of John of Exeter we are told, that "Godfrey Lucy made the vault with the aisles from the altar of the blessed Mary to the end (of the church), where he was buried outside the chapel of the blessed Virgin."

This last entry proves that the works of Bishop de Lucy were the eastern portions which lie between the altar wall of the Lady-chapel and the gable end of the church, the style of which is Early English, of an excellent character. This example is therefore worth examining as a well-dated building, as well as for its beauty.

[y] "Anno MCC. inchoata est et perfecta turris Wintoniensis Ecclesiæ." (Ann. p. 304.) "Anno MCCII. Dominus Wintoniensis Godefridus de Lucy constituit Confratriam quo reparatione Ecclesiæ Winton. duraturam usque ad quinque annos completos." (Ann. p. 305.)
"Godfridus Lucy ab altare beate Marie ad finem cum aliis voltam fecit ubi extra capellam beate Virginis humatus est, cum sedit annis xv." (John of Exeter, f. 5.) Wharton prints from an imperfect copy, and omits "*fecit*." That "aliis" is meant for "alis," appears from the "navem ecclesie cum aliis" under Wykeham.

Now in the general plan (at the end of this History), the plan of the crypt is indicated in a lighter tint, to shew its relation to the work above. It shews that the Norman cathedral, the high apse of·which terminated at Q, where the present gable stands, had a circular aisle round the end of it. This aisle, however, had towers R and S on each side, so that the external outline of this end of the church is reduced from a semicircle to a square. From the centre projected the chapel T, which may have been a lady chapel, or, as at Canterbury, may have been dedicated to the Holy Trinity. Such flanking towers were not unusual. At Canterbury the towers of St. Andrew and St. Anselm similarly flanked the Trinity chapel, but were beyond the line of the aisle to north and south. In the crypts of York the towers seem to have been placed as in the present example. It is probable that in the parts above the crypt the square outline would disappear. Indeed, as the outside of the wall is at present buried in the earth, we have no means of ascertaining exactly how far the towers are detached from the circular apse.

De Lucy's building extends from $L\,P$ eastward, and is distinguished by a different tint in the plan. The whole is nearly of the same height. It consists of three aisles or alleys, separated from each other by three arches on each side, and the central alley is very little higher than the lateral ones; each alley terminates eastward, with a chapel; of these the lateral chapels M and O still retain their eastern walls, but that portion of the central or Lady-chapel N, which projects beyond the others, is the work of Prior Hunton, at the end of the fifteenth century. This prior erected a crypt under his chapel, the vault of which is carried by two central pillars, and the vault is thus divided into six compartments. But this crypt is not confined to his own additional part of the chapel, for two of its compartments extend under the original Lady-chapel of De Lucy. The crypt of the latter being thus obliterated, it is not easy to discover whether De Lucy's chapel extended further east than the two lateral ones, or whether the three chapels were all of one length. From some indi-

Fig. 15. Capital, Lady chapel

cations that appear to mark the springing of the original east wall in Hunton's crypt, I am inclined to think that the chapels of De Lucy were all of the same extent.

The Lady-chapel itself presents a singular mixture of style. The north and south walls in their western compartment retain the rich Early English arcade and *alura* of De Lucy.

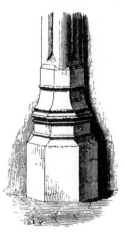

The eastern compartment on each side, as well as the east wall, have respectively a large Perpendicular window of seven lights, with transom and tracery of a peculiar kind of subordination, or rather interpenetration of patterns, well worth a careful study[z]. The vault is a complex and beautiful specimen of lierne work. The vaulting-shafts have capitals and bases (figs. 15. and 16.) of an unusual form, but very rich and appropriate. The western half of the chapel is fitted up with elaborately carved panelling, seats, and desks, and a skreen of separation, all of the most beautiful and perfect workmanship and design. The

Fig. 16.   Base, Lady-Chapel

lower part of the walls of the eastern half have been painted, and the remains of the painting still exist. These paintings have been minutely represented and described by Milner, in Carter's Specimens of Ancient Sculpture and Painting[a]. The western arch of separation between the Lady-chapel and the aisles that connect it with the choir of the cathedral retains the moldings of De Lucy, but not the form in which he left it, for to accommodate the vault of the fifteenth century it has been evidently taken down and reset in the shape of a four-centred arch.

The evidence upon which this chapel is dated was first pointed out by Milner. On the vault round the two central keys[b] "one representing the Almighty, the other the blessed Virgin, we find the following characters and rebuses: the letter T, the syllable *Hun*, the figure of a *ton* for *Thomas Hunton*, and the figure 1 for *prior*. In like manner we see the letter T, the syllable *silk*, a *steed* or horse, and the figure 1, for *Thomas Silkstede, prior*. In other parts of the chapel and cathedral we find the letter T, with a skein of *silk* twisted

---

[z] See Britton's Sections, Pl. xx.

[a] See also Milner's Winchester, vol. ii. p. 64.

[b] Milner's words are "the *groining* round the two center *orbs*."

round it, to denote the same person, with the *vine* and the *ton* (for *Wynton*). There are other proofs from the arms of Queen Elizabeth, daughter of Edward VI., and those of the Grey family, that the addition to this chapel was begun to be built whilst Hunton was prior, but that it was finished and ornamented by Silkstede. The latter fact is attested by an imperfect inscription under the portrait of this prior, which is still visible, with the insignia of his office over the piscina in the chapel, of which the following words are part: 𝔖ilkstede . . . . jussit quoque saxa polita, 𝔖umptibus ornari, 𝔖ancta 𝔐aria suis[c]." Prior Hunton held his office from 1470 to 1498, when he was succeeded by Silkstede, who died in 1524. This places the date of the additions to De Lucy's chapel at the end of the fifteenth century.

In the chapel is preserved the chair or *faldistorium* represented in fig. 17, which is said to have been that in which

Fig. 17. Queen Mary's Chair.

Queen Mary sat upon the occasion of her marriage with Philip of Spain, which ceremony was performed in this chapel[d].

    [c] Milner, vol. ii. p. 64.   [d] Milner, p. 65.

The south chapel (*O*) was fitted up as a chantry by Bishop Langton, who died in 1500. The woodwork is excessively rich and beautiful, and the vault still more elaborate than that of the Lady-chapel, for the panels between the ribs and liernes are covered with small tracery. This vault like the other has the rebuses of its builders : namely, as Milner explains them, the musical note termed a *long* inserted into a *ton* for *Langton;* a *vine* and *ton* for his see *Winton;* a *hen* sitting on a *ton* for his prior *Hunton;* and a *dragon* issuing out of a *ton*, which Milner declares himself unable to unriddle [e].

The external walls of De Lucy's work have evidently been erected complete before the arches and piers of its interior. The respond pier at *a* is entirely independent of the wall against which it rests, and the base moldings of this pier and of the wall are not bonded together, but straight-jointed, so as to shew subsequent work. The reason for this is explained by the relative position of this new work to the old, as shewn by the crypt, for it is clear that the external wall lies wholly outside the original chapel *T* and the aisle of the apse, and might therefore have been, as it probably was, erected without disturbing any other part of the building than the small towers *R* and *S*. When the external wall was finished, the chapel *T* and the aisle of the apse were taken down to the level of the pavement, leaving the crypt as to this day; and the walls of the old chapel served to carry the Early English piers of the new work. The arches that separate the chapels from the aisles are richly molded, and belong to the second portion of the work. A gradual progression of workmanship may be observed in the moldings in accordance with this account. In fig. 37, (at the end of this history,) I have assembled all the principal arch-moldings of the cathedral. *A* is the mold of the arcades that decorate the ground wall of these aisles ; *B* the mold of certain trefoil-headed arches that are placed against the upper part of the north and south walls of the Lady-chapel; *C* is the mold of the great arches that separate the aisles, and *D* that of the arches that divide the chapels *M* and *O* from the aisles. It will be seen that the two former profiles which belong to the walls are more rude in their distribution than the two latter that belong to the arches and vaults ; in fig. 38, *D E* are capi-

[e] Milner, p. 63. This chapel is also assigned to Langton by Godwin. " Capellam construxit ab australi parte ecclesiæ suæ Wintoniensis in cujus medio conditus jacet sub marmoreo tumulo elegantissimo."

tals, and in fig. 39, *B C* are base-molds from this part of
the church. The plan of a pier is shewn in fig. 5, above.
At *T* is a large slab of gray marble, without inscription, probably to mark the place of interment of Bishop de Lucy, for
John of Exeter has told us that he was buried outside the
lady chapel, under his vault; in accordance with the usual
practice of burying a founder in his work. By a slight confusion in the tradition, the vergers used to exhibit this tomb as
that of King Lucius[f].

The architecture of this
early specimen of the style
is remarkably elegant. It
has been well illustrated in
Mr. Britton's plates. The
doorway shewn in fig. 18
may be taken as a specimen.
It is one of those which lead
from the aisles to the small
turret staircases at their east
ends.

The peculiar arrangement
of these low eastern aisles
may be compared with those
of the cathedrals of Hereford, Salisbury, Chichester,
St. Alban's, Wells, and Exeter. Of these Winchester
is the most extensive, and
Hereford the earliest[g]. The
low eastern work of Here-
ford consists of two com-
partments of pointed Nor-
man, leading to an Early

Fig. 18.   Door north of Lady-Chapel

English Lady-chapel, and flanked by low Decorated transepts.
The distribution of the piers in the low eastern work of Wells
is peculiar complex, and produces a beautiful effect. It appears
to me to have been contrived with the especial purpose of facili-
tating the circulation of the processions, for which all these
aisles were formed. Gervase has told us[h] that care was taken

[f] Vide Milner, vol. ii. p. 62.

[g] Romsey seems to have had a similar
eastern addition, which would be earlier

than Hereford.

[h] Arch. Hist. of Cant., p. 61.

to accommodate them in the eastern aisles of Canterbury. William of Worcester applies the term "via processionum" to eastern aisles[i], and in English vocabularies they are called the "procession path[j]." In most of our larger churches, however, eastern additions are raised as high in the centre as the choir itself, as at Canterbury, Rochester, Ely, &c.

The portion of the church which lies between De Lucy's work, and the Norman central tower and transept, is of a most curiously mixed description. Three pier-arches on each side extend eastward from the tower; two of broader span then follow, one on each side, inclined to each other so as to give an irregular polygonal form to the east end[k]; and at the east is a double arch which carries the gable, and divides the presbytery from the low eastern aisles. The piers of these arches will be seen by the plan to rest upon the walls of the Norman crypt. The western piers of De Lucy's work, however, having been erected at first so as to stand clear of the Norman apse, were supported on supplemental piers erected in the crypt below. At *U* there still remains the stump of one of the Norman piers. Its simple base is shewn at *A*, fig. 39 (at the end of this history). It stands immediately over the crypt pier, and it shews that there were four of these cylinders in the curve of the apse. If the whole of the piers of the Norman choir stood thus immediately over the centre of their corresponding crypt piers, there would have been four pier arches in the straight part of the choir, and five in the curved part, instead of the present arrangement of three in the straight part, and four in the polygonal walls. But these arches must have been narrower than those of the nave and transept. The present compartments are about equal in breadth to those of the nave.

The plan of the piers of the choir is shewn in fig. 4. above, and in fig. 6. is the plan of one of the three small eastern piers that carry the gable. But the manner in which the arches of the east end join these piers, and those of De Lucy's work, is somewhat curious, and I have therefore inserted the following sketch to explain this arrangement.

---

[i] "Spacium sive via processionum a retro altaris principalis coram capellam Sanctæ Mariæ, &c."—W. Worcestre, p. 242.

[j] For example, see "The Nomenclator of A. Junius," by John Higins. 1585. p. 307.

[k] This convergence of the walls serves to contract the central alley of the church to the breadth of De Lucy's middle aisle, which breadth was determined by the walls of the old Lady-chapel below. The artifice resembles that of the eastern end of Canterbury. Arch. Hist. of Cant., p. 60.

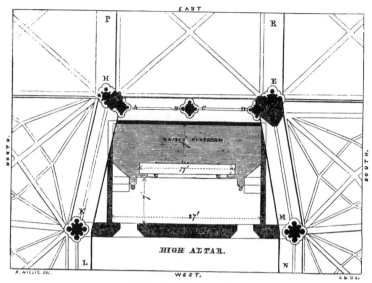

Fig 19.   Plan of East end of Choir.

H E are the western piers of De Lucy; *A B D* the small
eastern piers of the choir; *K* and *M* the eastern piers of the
straight wall of the same.   Now the arch that connects *K*
and *H* rests upon and springs from the abacus of *H*, and is
so united with it, that, viewed from the north side aisle, it
appears to carry on the arcade of De Lucy's work in a regular
sequence.   The arch *P H* is succeeded in order by *H K*
and *K L*.   The moldings of course are different.   As for the
arch *A B*, it springs from a higher level than *H K*, and its
moldings are made to abut, and interpenetrate with those of
the arch *K H*, with that peculiar method that the Gothic
masons delighted in.   The abacuses of the pillars *A B D* are
higher than those of *H* and *K*, because the former stand upon
a high wall that serves as a screen of separation between the east
end of the choir and the low eastern aisles.   The eastern face
of the wall is ornamented with tabernacles of rich Decorated
character.   In the figure of arch-moldings, (at the end of this
history,) *E* is the arch-mold of the two eastern arches *A B* and
C D, *F* is that of the north arch *H K*; and it will be seen at
once that, although not exactly the same, they are the work of
the same period.   But *G* is the arch-mold of the southern
arch *F M*, and this is wholly different, and as we shall see,
subsequent.   The manner in which this arch joins the

piers E and D, is wholly different from that just described, as the junction of the opposite and corresponding arch with the piers A and H. Instead of resting upon the abacus of E, and interpenetrating with $D C$, an additional pier F has been erected, joining together the piers D and E, and receiving the arch $M F$, the span of which is thus made less than that of the opposite arch, and its moldings are freed from interference with those of $C D$, while the whole work is rendered more substantial. It is easy to discover that the piers H and A were once quite separate. But at present the interstice between them is filled up with a mass of masonry, G, which now connects them. It seems therefore that when the polygonal east end was first undertaken, it was intended to adopt the system on the north side, and that the eastern arches and first northern arch were built as we now see them. Perhaps the southern arch was built too, and failed; at any rate, the present southern arch is of subsequent work, and erected, as I have explained, on a stronger and better plan; and the detached pillars at A and H were then bolstered by the way which I have described.

The other pier-arches of the choir have the molding marked H in the figure of arch-molds, very similar to G. That these arches were subsequent to the eastern work is plain, from the way in which this arch L joins the arch K. The latter arch, and the wall above it, rests upon the pier K, so as to shew that they were fairly erected upon it; the arch L and its wall merely abut against the others, as subsequent work would naturally do. On the leads of the north aisle we may observe that the eastern part of the work includes the buttress which stands on the pier K, and the seam between the two pieces of masonry lies between that buttress and the next western window. Although the succession of the works is thus plain, the exact period of their erection is not so easy to determine, in the total absence of any documents.

The work must have gone on slowly, and was probably carried up at the expense of the monastery, and not by any particular benefactor, therefore it has passed unrecorded. The piers are Decorated in form; the most easterly at V (in the general plan) is of older workmanship than the other three, although their capitals and bases are molded alike. From its excentric position upon the crypt pier below, it might have been erected without disturbing the Norman pier, which stood on the centre of that pier, and thus the polygonal end may have been built without taking down more than the circular apse of the Norman choir to begin with. For as the side aisles of this choir, which we shall presently examine, are the undoubted work of Bishop Fox, who held the see from 1500 to 1528; and the Decorated piers may be dated at 1320; it follows that about two hundred years elapsed from the beginning to the end of the work, and it is not likely that the monks were destitute of a choir or a roof to their high altar all this while. As in many other cases, I believe that they proceeded for their own convenience gradually, taking down only as much of the old building as they thought themselves able to replace with the funds in hand, or in prospect, at the time.

On each side of the choir of St. Alban's there still remains three compartments of the original low vaulted Norman aisles, although the piers and pier-arches are of lofty Decorated work. In fact, Norman piers are so much thicker than the succeeding ones, as I have above remarked, in chap. II., that it becomes possible to cut down the front portions of such piers and pier arches, so as to leave room for the erection of their thinner successors, without endangering the fall of the aisles of the older work, which, notwithstanding this loss of dimensions, is still strong enough to stand alone[1]. I imagine, therefore, that the Norman side aisles of our choir at Winchester were so treated, and that they were allowed to stand until the time of Fox; the Decorated piers and arches having been erected in front of them a century and a half before. The figures 10 and 11 above, shew the possibility of this. The manner in which the work of the side aisles now joins to the Norman work of the transept, confirms this view of the question. This junction is effected on the south side of the compartment J, (see general plan,) and on the north side of its opposite compartment W. The external wall of the side aisles of the choir is most richly decorated with moldings and panel-work, with noble windows, in the best Perpendicular style, and its vault is considerably higher than that of the Norman side aisles, indeed it reaches nearly as high as the roof of the Norman triforium. This Norman vault, then, is cut down vertically on the south side of J, and on the north side of W, and the Perpendicular wall, instead of stopping at b and c, as would usually be the

[1] It must be remembered, that the arches and piers so sliced have been previously disencumbered of the weight of the clerestory wall.

case, is carried on in front of and in close contact with this truncated Norman vault, so as to join the transept pier. This arrangement is shewn by the different tints on the plan, which are given to the Norman walls and the Perpendicular walls respectively.

The sketch (fig. 20.) is taken from the floor of the triforium of *W,* looking north-east. It shews the outer face of the Perpendicular wall in question at *A*, and the Norman wall of the triforium at *B*. It must be remarked, that a window is inserted in this compartment of the side aisles, similar to those in its other severies or ciboria. This would seem to indicate an ulterior plan for removing altogether the Norman eastern aisles of the transepts.

I have already stated that the Perpendicular side aisles are higher than the Norman, consequently this Perpendicu-

Fig. 20. Masonry in Triforium in South Transept.

lar window rises and shews part of its head in the Norman triforium, as in the figure; and by looking down, it will be seen that it is completely finished on this side, although in close contact with the truncated surface of the Norman vault. If the Norman aisles were now to be taken down to the plain surface of the masonry, the entire window would be found complete, like those of the neighbouring bays. Here then we have a case precisely similar to that I have suggested, as the mode in which the works of the entire choir were carried on, and which may be thus described :—

The Norman apse was first taken down about 1320, and the polygonal termination substituted. Then, perhaps thirty years afterwards, the Norman clerestory and triforium of the straight part of the choir was removed, and its piers and pier-arches reduced in front, as I have described, so as to make room for the present piers, pier-arches, and clerestory.

Next, under Bishop Fox, about 1510, the Norman aisles

were taken down, and the present aisles erected. If the scheme had been carried on in accordance with the views of the projectors, the eastern aisles of the transepts would probably have followed, and have been replaced by other arrangements in the style of the day.

In this account I have no historical documents to guide me in fixing the dates. The moldings of the polygonal termination (see figures at the end) are Decorated in style, and resemble those of the lantern and other works at Ely, known to have been carried on from 1322 to 1328. Also the tabernacle work of the east face of the choir wall is of the same period. Hence I have placed the date of the polygonal part at about 1320. The arrangement of the compartment also resembles that of the lantern at Ely, and of the Decorated choir of Lichfield, consisting as they all do of two stages only, pier-arch and clerestory, and having a gallery or *alura* under the clerestory window, with a pierced balustrade in front. The tracery of the windows is, however, Perpendicular. But this tracery has been evidently inserted into the polygonal face of the north compartment, for the molding of the half monial at the jamb differs from that of the middle monials. What the east window may have been we know not, the gable that now stands having been rebuilt by Bishop Fox, whose device is to be found upon it. The entire design of the choir has been copied from that compartment which was first executed. Hence it happens that its moldings *G H* (see figure of arch-molds at end) appear later than the style of the composition. I am inclined to fix this part of the work at the beginning of Bishop Edingdon's period.

Edingdon held the see from 1345 to 1366, and, as we shall see in the next chapter, the great work of the nave was begun by him, and occupied his successors, Wykeham, Beaufort, and Waynflete. This may account for the delay that took place between the erection of the central part of the choir and of its side aisles; for the more important work of the nave, rendered necessary by its ruinous condition, must have absorbed all the attention and funds. There are several details in the clerestory of the choir that resemble similar ones in Edingdon's work. For example, the cusps of the window tracery are terminated with flowers instead of being simply pointed, a fact which I shall presently shew will serve to identify Edingdon's work at the west end of the nave. The

tracery of the clerestory windows in the choir is greatly in-
ferior to that of Fox in its side aisles, or to that of Wykeham
in the nave, but has many points of resemblance to that of
Edingdon in the nave. The side aisles of the choir are
identified with Fox by his badges and emblems, which
abound in this part of the work. The east end gable is
crowned by his statue resting on his emblem, the pelican.
The north corbel of the hoodmold of this east window is a
most characteristic portrait bust of a bishop, evidently Fox,
from the resemblance to his head above. The flying buttresses,
which the jointing of the masonry prove to have been subsequent insertions into the wall of the clerestory, have also
the pelican of Fox carved upon them. The insertion of these
buttresses is explicable if we recollect that the walls of the
clerestory have just been attributed to Bishop Edingdon. The
roof of the choir is of wood framed to imitate stone, but
the vault of the side aisles is a fine piece of stone lierne work.
These aisles, as may be seen from the account given in these
pages, present a curious and instructive mixture of style. Thus
the pier H (fig.19.) receives an Early English pier-arch $P\,H$ on
the east side, a Decorated pier-arch $H\,K$ on the west, an Early
English vault and ribs on the north-east side, and a set of
Perpendicular vault-ribs on the north-west. The rib that runs
northwards from this pier is halved, and has Early English
moldings on one side, and Perpendicular on the other. Also
the pier-arch $H\,K$ has a Perpendicular wall-rib running parallel to its Decorated moldings on its north side.

I have hitherto employed the word choir in its architectural
sense. But in this cathedral the ancient Norman arrangement
being retained, the actual "choir of the monks," the place
where the stalls are fixed, is under the tower, and that which is
termed the choir, is proved distinctly to be the presbytery. The
high altar was fixed originally between the extreme pillars
$K\,M$ (fig. 19,) and the shrine of Swithun and the other saints
appear to have stood behind it. A lofty and magnificent reredos now extends from pillar to pillar, immediately backing
the altar; and the space behind it to the east, including the
polygonal part of the choir, is thus cut off and separated; a
door on each side the altar leads to this space.

This was the "feretory," a place for the feretra or shrines of
the patron saints. The arrangement is analogous to that of
many other cathedrals. Unfortunately, the date of this reredos

is not preserved, and there are no devices to lead us to fix it with any precision, save only that its style indicates late work, and it may therefore be assigned to the latter end of the fifteenth century. The lateral enclosure of the choir is effected by screens of stone tracery, which bear initials, mottos, devices, and a date. We have in different parts the initials of Fox and his motto, 𝔈𝔰𝔱 𝔇𝔢𝔬 𝔊𝔯𝔞𝔠𝔦𝔞, in black letter, the initials of Cardinal Beaufort and his motto, IN DOMINO CONFIDO, and the initials W. F. and motto, SIT LAUS DEO, of some unknown benefactor. There is also the date 1525. Under each pier-arch upon the screen is placed a mortuary chest, also the work of Bishop Fox[m].

The feretory, which is cut off from the rest of the choir by the high reredos, was once of course visible from the choir; at the extreme east end there are still to be seen the ruins of its ancient arrangement, shewn in the plan, (fig.19.) The sides of this chapel are at present occupied by two chantry chapels, that of Gardiner on the north, and of Fox on the south. At the east part is a raised platform, seven feet broad, extending quite across. Its upper surface is now three feet above the floor, but was originally much higher; steps at each end gave access to this upper surface, and in front there are the remains of a hollow place, which, from the piers and other indications that remain on the floor, evidently had an arcade in front of it, over which the pavement of the platform extended so as to make its breadth about ten feet in the whole.

This platform probably sustained the shrine of St. Swithun, and also those of SS. Birinus, Edda, and Ethelwold, or of some of them, for these are recorded as the especial patrons of the

[m] There are six of these chests in all: three on each side, made of wood, carved, painted, and gilt, and designed in the cinque cento style, which in the time of Fox was making its appearance in England. The persons whose remains were by him deposited in them appear from the inscriptions, but the bones which they now contain can hardly be identified with the inscriptions, because it is known that these chests, or at least some of them, were opened in the civil war, and their contents scattered about the church. The remains were collected afterwards, and deposited in two of the chests. The entire inscriptions and other particulars may be found in Milner, (vol. ii. p. 47.) The names inscribed on the chests in order, are, beginning from the altar on the north side, and returning to it again on the south :—

(1.) Rex Kyngils. Adulphus Rex.
(2.) Kenulphus Rex. Egbertus Rex.
(3) and (4.) "In hac et altera e regione cista reliquæ sunt Cnuti et Rufi regum Emmæ reginæ, Winæ et Alwyni Episcoporum."
(5.) Edmundus Rex.
(6.) Edredus Rex.
In the mixture of bones in chests (3) and (4) we have the remains of the confusion which existed in the time of Henry de Blois, see art. 24, ch. 1. above; and these chests now carry an additional inscription to the effect that in 1661 they were made the receptacles of the promiscuous mixture of the bones of princes and prelates which had been scattered by the sacrilegious barbarism of 1642.

church. Whether the arcade below was appropriated to the reception of smaller relics we cannot tell. It was usual to raise up the shrines of saints, and leave a free space under them. Indeed the most common way was to place the shrine of a notable saint in an isolated position in the midst of the feretory, with open arcades below, as in the case of Edward the Confessor, Thomas à Becket, &c.

The east end of this platform is bounded by a wall, the eastern face of which has been already described as being ornamented with tabernacles of Decorated work. This wall is about twelve feet high on the side next to the low aisles of De Lucy, and the floor under the platform is carried by a small vault, the entrance to which is by a low arch in the eastern face of the wall under the range of tabernacles. This vault[n] is supposed to be that which is designated as the *Holy Hole* in the records (art. 24, ch. 1. above). There are nine tabernacles, and in each two pedestals; under these pedestals there still remain the inscribed names of the persons represented by the images that once stood upon them[o].

The Norman crypt is at present filled up with earth to a considerable height, and is moreover obstructed in all directions by masses of brickwork raised for the reception of coffins, for the water lies so near the surface that it is not only impossible to bury under the pavement of the original crypt, but it has also been thought advisable thus to cover up the lower parts of the pillars and walls. The structure of the crypt appears to terminate westward at the eastern piers of the tower. But the raised platform above the crypt, which includes the presbytery and its aisles, and all the eastern part of the church, is also extended under the central tower, and beyond it to the

[n] The position of this vault, and its relation to the pavement of the choir and feretory, may be understood from Britton's sections, pl. 2, fig. 4. His plate 23 shews the eastern elevation of the wall, with its range of tabernacles, and the arch of the Holy Hole below them, also shewn in one of Coney's spirited etchings in the Monasticon. In pl. 22, Britton, is an elevation of one of the tabernacles. These tabernacles are beautiful specimens of Edwardian work, and well deserve study. They may be compared with the similar work in the Lady-chapel of Ely, which was begun in 1321, and occupied about thirty years.

[o] Kyngilsus rex (s). S. Birinus episcopus. Kynwaldus rex (s). Egbertus rex (s).

Adulphus rex filius ejus (s). Aluredus rex (s). Edwardus rex senior (b). Athelstanus rex (b). Dominus Jesus. Sancta Maria. Edredus rex (s). Edgar rex (b). Emma regina (s). Alwynus episcopus. Ethelredus rex (b). S. Edwardus rex filius ejus (b). Canutus rex (s). Hardicanutus rex filius ejus (s). Comparing this list with that of John of Exeter, I find it to include all the kings before the Conquest that were either buried in Winchester cathedral or were benefactors to the same. I have marked those who received sepulture there with (s), and those who were benefactors only, with (b). Of Alfred, or Alured, he records that he was first buried in this church, and afterwards translated by his son to the new monastery.

second pillar westward from the tower pier. At this point a flight of steps, with an intermediate landing, or "half pace," at *Z*, (see general plan at end,) connects the raised pavement of the choir with the lower level that prevails in the nave and transepts. This lower level also joins to the higher by means of lateral steps at *Y* in the side aisles of the nave, and similarly by steps at *X* access is given from the transepts to the side aisles of the presbytery. As the compartment *J* in the east aisle of the north transept, and the compartment *K* in the side aisle of the presbytery, are thus on the two different levels respectively, the door of the crypt is conveniently placed in the south side of *J*.

The stalls extend from the western corners of the eastern tower-piers to the first pier of the nave, and are terminated on the north side by a rich pulpit of wood, which bears the name of its donor, " Thomas Silkstede, prior[p]," on different parts of it. The woodwork of the stalls is exceedingly rich and beautiful. It has, however, been subjected to various alterations, that may be easily detected upon examination. They are of early Decorated work, and their canopies and gables bear considerable resemblance to that of the tomb of Edmund Crouchback, in Westminster Abbey, as Milner has most truly observed[q]. This would place their date about the year 1296. The desks and stools in front of the upper range bear the initials of Henry VIII., of Bishop Stephen Gardiner, Dean W. Kingsmill, and the date 1540. Formerly a " pulpitum," or roodloft, extended from pillar to pillar of the nave over the landing (*Z*) of the steps leading to the choir. This bore the great cross of Stigand, described in a previous chapter[r]. The space between this and the stalls was probably occupied by chapels and altars. The chantry chapel of Edingdon still remains on the south of the landing at 3, and the state of the piers on the north side shews that they were formerly covered by some wood or stone work now removed; for, as we shall presently see, the pillars of the nave, originally Norman, have all been cased, and altered into Perpendicular. But in these piers the upper part only is so changed, and the lower still shews the old Norman work, which it was not practicable or necessary so to change at the time the alteration was made, because they were then concealed by some

[p] He was prior from 1498 to 1524.
[q] Milner, ii. p. 36.   Britton, pl. 14, has an elevation of the stalls.
[r] See chap. i. art. 18. above.

decorations connected with the western entrance of the choir. This, whatever it was, seems to have been removed after the Reformation; and in the reign of Charles I. a screen of the composite order was erected, as a mere wall of separation, at the west end of the stalls, between the two first piers of the nave on each side; for in this cathedral the organ is not placed over the west door of the choir, but under the tower-arch of the north transept, consequently no gallery is required, as usual in other cathedrals, and a single wall is sufficient for a screen. The classical screen is now replaced by one more in accordance with the style of the building, the work of the late Mr. Garbett.

Before quitting this portion of the church, I must mention two chapels formed in the eastern aisles of the south transept, by screens of stone tracery work. The south is called Silk-

stede's chapel, because the letters of his Christian name, Thomas, are carved on the cornice or crest of the stone screen, but in such a manner that the M. A., the monogram of his patroness, the Virgin Mary, are distinguished from the rest; together with the skein of silk which is the rebus of his surname. Fig. 21 is a lock of this chapel.

Fig. 21.   Lock of the Chapel

The bench, of which a portion is

Fig. 22.   Bench in South Transept.

Fig. 23   Iron-work, S Transept

shewn in fig. 22, is preserved in the south transept; from its rudeness of construction and its ornaments, it might be coeval with the transept itself; but I have not examined it with sufficient minuteness to give a decided opinion upon it.

The north chapel is remarkable for the elaborate and beautiful iron work with which the openings of its tracery are defended, of which a portion is represented in fig. 23.

CHAP. IV.

ON THE NAVE.

WE have now arrived at the nave of the church, which exhibits one of the most curious instances of transformation from one style of architecture to another that has been preserved to us. For although at present a complete and perfect specimen of the fourteenth and fifteenth centuries, it is yet in the heart and core of its structure from the ground to the roof the original Norman building commenced, if not completed, by Bishop Walkelin. To develope and explain the nature of this singular state of things is the object of the present chapter. For although it has been pointed out by Milner and subsequent writers, there are many particulars that appear to me to have escaped observation, and the whole process is so curious an example of the modes of proceeding in the middle ages, that it deserves a very minute examination. And first for the history.

In the will of Bishop Edingdon, (who held this see from 1345 to 1366,) he desires that a portion of his property shall be expended upon the completion of the nave of the Cathedral at Winchester which he had begun, &c.[s]

Which part of the nave he had so begun, history does not inform us, but we shall presently shew that it was at the west end. Edingdon was succeeded by William of Wykeham. It is not consistent with the plan which I have laid down for this short history to relate more of the events of

---

[s] By his will dated 1366 "præcepit, ut de bonis suis expenderetur ad perfectionem navis Ecclesiæ Cathedralis Winton, à se inchoatæ et ad subsidium domûs sive Can- thariæ de Edyngdon à se fundatæ."— Registr. Langham cited in Ang. Sac., tom. i. p. 317.

his life than are immediately connected with the works of the cathedral in question, and indeed the admirable and well known biography by Bishop Lowth, would in any case have rendered such a task superfluous. It appears that Wykeham (a native of Wykham in Hampshire) was recommended by his first patron, Nicholas Uvedale, governor of Winchester castle, to Bishop Edingdon, and by both was made known to Edward III.[t] He is proved to have been in Edingdon's service in 1352. He was placed in the king's service when about 22 or 23 years of age, and in 1356 was made clerk of all the king's works in his manors of Henle and Yeshamsted. In the same year he was appointed surveyor of the king's works at the castle, and in the park of Windsor[u].

William of Wykeham was elected bishop of Winchester 1366, consecrated Oct. 10, 1367, and immediately set about repairing all the episcopal buildings, and purchased the use of the stone quarries of Quarrer Abbey in the Isle of Wight. The abbot engaged to assist him as general director and surveyor of these preparations, and the bishop wrote circular letters to all the ecclesiastics of the island, both regular and secular, to desire them to send in as many workmen, carriages, and necessaries for the work, as they could supply him with at the demand and according to the directions of the abbot, all to be defrayed at his own expense[x].

---

[t] Lowth, p. 13, 17.

[u] By this patent he had powers given him to press all sorts of artificers, and to provide stone, timber, and all other materials and carriages. He had one shilling a day while he staid at Windsor, 2s. when he went elsewhere on his employment, and 3s. a week for his clerk.—Lowth, 18.

"Circa ann[m]. Dom[l]. 1359, Dominus Rex ad instigationem W. Wykeham Clerici in castro de Wyndshore, multa bona ædificia fecit prosterni et alia plura pulchra et sumptuosa ædificari; omnes fere lathomi et carpentarii per totam Angliam ad illam ædificationem fuerunt adducti, ita quod vix aliquis potuit habere aliquem bonum lathomum vel carpentarium nisi in abscondito propter regis prohibitionem."—Cronica MS. in Corp. Chr. Cantab. Lowth, 19.

Wykeham had also the sole direction of the building of Queenborough Castle (in insula de Shepeye.)—Lowth, 19.

On 10th July, 1359, he was constituted chief warden and surveyor of the king's castles of Windsor, Ledes, Dover, and Hadlam, and of the manors of Old and New

Windsor, &c. with powers to appoint all workmen, to provide materials, &c. . . .

In the next year workmen were impressed in London, and out of the several counties, for the works at Windsor.—Ashmole by Lowth, 22.

He held the deanery of St. Martin's le Grand, London, for 3 years, and rebuilt at his own expense "Claustrum domus capituli et corpus ecclesiæ."—MS. Coll. Winton; also Newcourt's Repertorium, i. 424 and 427, Rot. Pat. in Tanner Notit. 297.

Amongst other preferments enumerated by Lowth is, he was canon of Lincoln, 1362; had a prebend in York, 1362; in St. Stephen's, Westminster, 1363; archdeaconry of Northampton and Lincoln, and the prepositure of Wells, with prebend annexed, 1363.

[x] Lowth, 61, from MS. penes Dom. Epis. Wint.

The dates of the foundations of his two colleges at Oxford and Winchester are thus given by Chandler. . . .

Erexit enim titulum et posuit primum lapidem in Coll[o]. Wintoniensi in Oxoniâ,

In the year 1393, Wykeham held a fourth visitation of the monastery of his cathedral at Winchester, a principal object of the inquiry being the state and condition of the fabric, which was greatly out of repair, and the estates allotted to it very insufficient. The bishop ordered that the prior for the time being should pay £100 a year for seven years ensuing, and the sub-prior and convent 100 marks in like manner, for this service, over and above the profits of all estates so allotted, and all gifts and legacies. Soon after we find that the bishop relieved the prior and convent from the whole charge, and, with his usual generosity, took it entirely upon himself[y].

Some work had previously been carrying on at a great expense in the year 1371[z]. But Wykeham's work was undertaken in the year 1394[a], and entered upon in the beginning of the following year, upon certain conditions stipulated between him and the prior and convent[b], which will presently appear from his will.

He died on the 27th of September, A.D. 1404, leaving, as it appears, the work unfinished, but it was carried on and completed by his successors.

The few particulars which I have just extracted from Lowth serve to shew that this bishop was connected with Winchester from his youth, and also that he was essentially a practical man, and engaged in architectural works of the most extensive kind all his life. This gives an additional interest to the works in question, because we may imagine that the mode of proceeding was his own device, and that the designs were mainly due to him. Now although he is recorded by his biographers[c] as having erected the nave as we see it, it is

---

A.D. 1379, 3 Ric. II. The society made their public entrance into it 1386, April 14. Collegii B. Mariæ prope Civitatem Wintoniæ primi lapidis positio facta fuerat, Mar. 26, 1387, 11 Ric. II.; and the first entrance of the Society, post constructionem dicti Collegii, Mar. 28, 1393.— Brevis Cronica. Ang. Sac., tom. ii. p. 356.

The chapel of this college was dedicated and consecrated in 1395.—Reg. Wykeham in Lowth, p. 176.

Henry Chicheley, abp. of Canterbury, one of Wykeham's own scholars, whom he had himself seen educated in both his societies, following his master's great example, built a chantry and hospital at Higham Ferrers, and founded All Souls College at Oxford.

[y] I extract the whole of this account

from Lowth, (p. 192,) who quotes in confirmation the Harleian MS. No. 328. f. 12 for the visitation, and the Leger Book of the Church of Winton, No. 1. fol. 20.

[z] Lowth, (p. 194,) quotes Reg. Wykeham, part 3. a. fol. 47.

[a] Novam fabricam (Ecclesiæ Wynton) incepit die Mercurii prox. post festum omnium Sanctorum anno regni Regis Ric. II. xviii. (1394.)—MS. Coll. Winton. (Lowth, 195.)

[b] Lowth, (195,) quotes Leger Book of Winchester Church, No. 1. fol. 18, and the will.

[c] "Willelmus de Wykeham, qui navem Ecclesiæ cum aliis prout nunc cernitur renovari et voltari fecit."—John of Exeter, f. 5 b. Ang. Sac., tom. i. p. 286.

" Ecclesiam illam (Winchester cathe-

plain, from various evidences, that this assertion must be taken loosely, to mean that he had the greatest share in its construction. The best information concerning the exact state of the works at the time of his death, and the mode in which they were carried on, is furnished by his will, and accordingly I shall proceed to extract and translate all those portions of that document that relate to the cathedral. It is dated at South Waltham, July 24, 1403, about fifteen months before his death[d], and nine years after his part of the work was begun.

Item. I desire that my body be buried in the middle of a certain chapel by me newly erected on the south side of the nave of the cathedral church of Winchester.

Item. I will and ordain that my executors shall cause to be reconstructed the body or middle part of the aforesaid church, between the north and south aisles, from the west door of the choir downwards as far as the west end, in its walls, windows, and vault, handsomely and well, according to the form and manner of the new work of the aforesaid aisles now begun, and they shall also complete the said aisles through the same extent in length. And they shall expend upon the work as much as 2,500 marks, if so much be required for its completion in the form and manner above defined. It being premised, however, that the prior and convent of the church shall provide all the scaffold necessary and convenient for the work; also, that they shall freely and without charge permit lime and sand to be taken by the workmen sent by myself or my executors, from any part of the lands of the convent or of their tenants, where it is of the best quality; also, that the stones, lead, iron-work, timber, glass, or any other of the materials which the old building may yield entire, shall remain, and be employed in the new work.

And I will and ordain that the arrangement and conduct of the new work shall be entrusted to Master William Winford, and such others discreet, sufficient, and approved in their art, as may be chosen, if necessary, by my executors. Also, that Dominus Simon Membury, now supervisor and paymaster of the work, shall continue in the same offices under the supervision and controul of Brother John Wayte, monk of my said church, and at present controller of the work on the part of the prior and convent, so long as he shall continue in good health, but when he becomes unfit or unable to work, then the prior and convent shall appoint some other monk

dral) pluribus donis, viz. vestimentis de pannis auri aliisque jocalibus quàm hîc inseri possint mirificè decoravit; corpusque dictæ Ecclesiæ cum duabus alis et omnibus fenestris vitreis à magnâ Occidentali fenestrâ capitali usque ad campanile à fundo usque ad summum de novo reparavit et voltas in eisdem opere curioso con-

stituit . . . . . . cujus corpus jacet tumulatum in Oratorio B. M. V. in navi Ecclesiæ Cathedralis Wintoniensis quod ipse superstes ad honorem ejusdem Virginis fieri ordinavit."—Brevis Cronica, Ang. Sac., tom. ii. p. 356.

[d] It is printed at length in the original Latin in Lowth's Appendix, p. xxxii.

of the said church to succeed him as controller so long as the work shall last. And the payments shall be made from time to time, according to the discretion of the whole of my executors, or of any five at the least.

Item. I bequeath five hundred marks for the glazing of the windows both above and below of the south side of the aforesaid church by me repaired, to be done handsomely and well, according to the directions of my executors. And I desire that the glazing shall be begun at the west end of the church, with the new work there made by me, and carried on seriatim and in order, to the completing of all the windows of the south side of the said new work. And if then any portion of the sum remains, I will that it be expended upon the windows of the north aisle, beginning at the west end, with the first window of the new work by me made, and so going on eastward as I have already ordained, from the south side, &c. . . . . .

The west front of the present nave, together with two windows and the three buttresses that belong to them on the north side of the north aisle, and also one window on the south side of the south aisle, are very different in design from the rest of the work. This portion may therefore be attributed to Bishop Edingdon. And it will be remarked, that in Wykeham's will just recited, he carefully desires that the windows of each aisle are to be glazed, beginning at the westernmost window of the part which he himself has erected, thereby excluding the windows that had been erected by his predecessor, and probably glazed by him.

From the will it seems that at the time that document was written the body of the church was incomplete, or remained to be erected, that the aisles were not finished, and that the windows were not glazed. Now in giving directions for the glazing he begins with the south side, and desires that the windows of that side, both above and below, (that is, both of aisle and clerestory,) shall be first done. I infer therefore that the south side was erected under his own superintendance, and nearly completed. And as he then proceeds to the windows of the north aisle of the new work " by me made," it seems that the north aisle was begun. As the work of the aisles necessarily includes the piers, pier-arches, and all the lower part of the body or central portion of the church, the parts left for his executors to complete must have been the clerestory wall of the north side, and the vault. This view is perfectly borne out by the building itself. For the works of the south side, as I shall presently shew, are carried on upon a different system from those of the north, retaining more of the original Norman structure, and this system appears to have been abandoned before the north side was begun. As to the vault of the nave, its bosses, as well as the tablet below the triforium, have the arms and busts of Cardinal Beaufort and of his father, together with their devices, the white hart chained, &c., as also the lily of Bishop Waynflete, intermingled with the arms and busts of the founder, Wykeham[e]. Beaufort and Waynflete were the immediate successors of Wykeham, and these devices would shew that the sculpture at least, of the nave and of its vault, was not completed for nearly fifty years after Wykeham's death. Now the work which I have attributed to Edingdon includes only the outer wall, marked with a different tint in the plan. The vaults of the side aisles of these compartments, namely, two in the north aisle and one in the south, belong to the work of Wykeham, and the piers and pier-arches of his work extend completely to the west end, and include the two responds or half piers from which the western pier-arches spring. These responds join the great west wall with a straight joint, and are not apparently bonded thereto.

The view in p. 60. represents the outside of the wall of the north aisle at the west end. It shews four buttresses all different from each other. The left hand buttress, however, is similar to all the others on this side of the Church. In the other three there is a general similarity, but the number of set-offs is greater by one, than in the left hand buttress, which we may call Wykeham's.

Our view also shews three windows, of which the left hand one (or Wykeham's) is of a much more elegant and peculiar design than that of the other two, which are singularly heavy, and from the extreme depth of their exterior moldings have a most cavernous and gloomy appearance. These differences were first pointed out by the acuteness of Milner[f], and shewn by him to indicate the respective works of Wykeham and Edingdon. The little north door may be remarked as the one opposite to which the chapel of St. Swithun used to stand[g]. A set-off in the wall above Edingdon's windows is seen, which marks the upper boundary of his remaining work. The pinnacles and upper set-off of his buttresses were added by Wykeham, and resemble the others. But the last buttress and pinnacle apparently remain in the state in which Edingdon left them.

e Milner, p. 24.   f P. 17.   g See ch. i. art. 6. above.

Fig. 24.   Three Bays, North Aisle of Nave.

The moldings of the windows in question, both within and without, afford a very useful test of the different powers of the artists that designed them.

In figure 25, *D* belongs to the Edingdon windows, and *C* to the Wykeham windows of the side aisles.   Externally, (on the lower half of the figure,) the arch-mold of the first consists of two singularly broad and shallow casements or hollow moldings, that of the second has a small casement, and a double ressant molding, sometimes called a brace, from its resemblance to that character ⌣.   The first joins the face of the tracery by a simple square nook, the second by a graceful elliptical casement, which detaches the fillet effectually.   The wall is also greatly reduced in thickness, and as the glass is

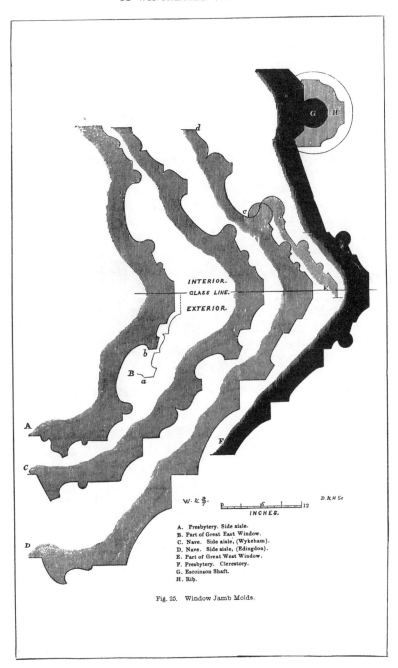

INTERIOR.

GLASS LINE.

EXTERIOR.

W. & T.

D. & H Sc

INCHES.

A. Presbytery. Side aisle.
B. Part of Great East Window.
C. Nave. Side aisle, (Wykeham).
D. Nave. Side aisle, (Edingdon).
E. Part of Great West Window.
F. Presbytery. Clerestory.
G. Escoinson Shaft.
H. Rib.

Fig. 25. Window Jamb Molds.

fixed in both windows at the same distance from the inside face, the difference is wholly thrown upon the exterior effect. The two hollow molds of Edingdon's exterior arch were probably copied from the window of the clerestory of the choir, (*F*, fig. 25.[h])

In the interior the moldings also differ. Edingdon's begins with a brace-molding, and Wykeham's with a triple group. The monial-mold of the first is more complex than that of the second, and the boutells of the first are flanked by a fillet and sharp edge, which is wanting in the second.

The base moldings given to the shafts of Edingdon's work in the interior are entirely different from those of Wykeham. In the figure of bases at the end, *I* is Edingdon's, *K* and *L* are Wykeham's. The first consists of two slender casements only. The last has, in addition to a broader casement below, a molding above, which is wholly wanting in the first. In the figure, *L* is the mold of Wykeham's wall-side shafts, and *K* the mold that belongs to the great shafts of his piers. In figure 26. a part of the wall is sketched from the west end, where Wykeham's work unites with Edingdon's. *A* is one of Wykeham's

Fig. 26   Bases of Shafts of West end of Nave.

shafts with the complex mold, and *B* one of Edingdon's with the simpler mold.

Another difference is to be found in the heads of the panels in the two works, and also in the arch-heads of the lights in the windows. The following figures respectively represent the arch-heads of the two works, fig. 27. of Edingdon and fig. 28. of Wykeham. The points of the cusps in Edingdon's work are decorated each with a small leaf. In Wykeham's work they are each plain.

In Wykeham's panels the masonry of the panels itself is carefully finished, and the same stones serve in fact for the ground of the panel and for the moldings ; but in Eding-

[h] See p. 61. above.

Fig. 27. Head of Panels and Lights in Edingdon's work.

Fig. 28. Head of Panels and Lights in Wykeham's work

don's panels the monials and tracery only are framed of good masonry, and the panels are filled up with rough ashlar.

Now by means of these tests it becomes perfectly evident that the great west window, with the western porches, constitutes a part of the same work as the lateral walls and windows that have just been attributed to Edingdon, and that these works are totally different from the portion that belongs to Wykeham. The flowered cusps are employed throughout the entire west window, from the panels below to the head above, and also throughout the western porches, as well as throughout the windows of the walls of the side aisles at the three western compartments already mentioned, and also for the two western windows of those aisles. The small slender base prevails throughout these parts alone, and runs all through the western porches. The moldings of the great west window only differ from those of Edingdon's side aisles in the manner shewn in figure 25. They are identical from d to c, but from c to E, although the moldings are alike, those of the great window are thrown a little farther outwards from the jamb, to allow apparently for the greater magnitude of the work. From all these indications I am confident that the west front forms one design with the two compartments on the north and the one on the south, and that it must be therefore attributed to Edingdon. I am inclined to think that the gable and turrets were not finished by him; and there are curious indications of change of plan about them, which are very difficult to disentangle. The external jamb of the great window has exactly the same moldings as those of Edingdon's side-aisle windows (*D*, fig. 25,) namely, the two great casement moldings. Fig. 29. represents the jamb moldings and impost of the west window, and if we follow these moldings up the jamb to the impost point, we shall find that the outer casement *A* is stopped there by means of a cap molding, and that the inner one *B* is only carried over the arch-head. It may be supposed, therefore, that this arch having been left unfinished at Edingdon's death, the deep cavernous effect already alluded to had already been objected to by his successor Wykeham, and that therefore the outer casement molding was thus disposed of when

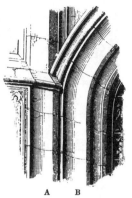

A B

Fig. 29. Jamb Moldings and Impost of West Window.

the gable was carried up. The flowered cusps, however, extend to the tracery of the spandrels, but not to that of the tracery of the triangular gable above. They were probably abandoned by Wykeham when he began his great work, on account of the additional expense and trouble they occasioned. I have already mentioned that they are to be found in the clerestory windows of the presbytery, whence they were probably copied like the double casement moldings, when the west end was begun[i]. The design of the west window is singularly simple, reducing itself to the merest stone grating. Divided into three great vertical compartments by principal monials, each of these is again split into three by secondary monials. Seven transoms divide the space into eight horizontal compartments. But the door in the centre and the arch-heads of the lights disturb the regularity of those at the top and bottom of the window. The window sill coincides with the second transom from the bottom, consequently we have panels below it and lights above it; then we find four rows of nine lights each, all alike, and above these the arch-head, which can scarcely be said to be filled with tracery, so completely does the grating-like character pervade it. In fact, in the central group of lights the grating extends to the very top, as well as in the middle of each great lateral division, the only attempt at curvilinear tracery being the filling up of the two side subordinate compart-

---

i Britton, pl. 4, has an exterior view of the west end, and in his Chronological Antiquities, vol. v., an interior view of the same.

ments of each great lateral division ; and this, as it happens to coincide with the similar parts of Wykeham's aisle and clerestory windows, has been thought by some writers enough to identify the two as the works of the same person.

It appears from recent investigations that the west front of the Norman cathedral extended about forty feet in advance of the present one. Some raised ground in front of the western doors, and remains of walls in an adjacent garden, have long given rise to an opinion that this might be the case; but Mr. Owen Carter has lately excavated the ground and traced the foundations, which are shewn in a light tint in my plan, and which I have copied from a sketch, for which I am indebted to the kindness of that gentleman. These foundations shew a wall of 128 feet from north to south, and 12 feet thick, with returns at each end, of the same thickness, 60 feet in length. At their eastern ends the walls again turn at right angles, and meet the present side aisles at 17 feet from each corner. Within the parallelogram thus partially traced two other walls run from east to west, at a distance of 36 feet from each other. At

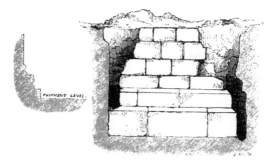

Fig. 30. Base of West Towers.

the north-east angle *c*, the excavation uncovered the plinth represented in the margin. This plinth consists of two plain faces with chamfers, and corresponds exactly in profile and in level with the Norman plinth of the south transept.

The figure on the left side shews the relative level of the pavement and base in the interior of the north transept, as nearly as can be indicated, for the level of the pavement varies considerably.

In a garden adjoining the west end of the cathedral, part of the south-west angle of the walls still remains, to a consider-

able height above the ground, as shewn by the darker tint at
d e f. But this is a mere mass of rubble stripped of ashlar.

These foundations must either have belonged to two western towers, or to a kind of western transept; and this construction, whatever it was, having been in all probability either
left unfinished or threatening ruin, Edingdon was induced
to take it down, and replace it by the present west front.
Similarly at Gloucester cathedral the western towers were
removed, and replaced by the present Perpendicular west
front at the beginning of the fifteenth century.

I shall now endeavour to explain the *transformation* of the
nave from Norman architecture to Perpendicular; and I use
this word advisedly instead of *rebuilding,* for it will be shewn
that the Norman core still remains in the piers and walls up
to the parapet, and in many places the Norman ashlaring as
well. Many of the piers
on the south side, namely,
the eight westerly ones,
including the half pier, retain the Norman ashlar-
ing, upon which the new
moldings have been
wrought. The Norman
arches still remain behind
the triforium. Norman
shafts still remain above
the present vault, as
shewn by the annexed
sketch, taken between the
stone vault of the nave
and the wooden roof, and

Fig. 31   Norman Shaft in Roof.

representing one of the pockets, as they are called, of Wykeham's vault. Lastly, on the outside of the clerestory the
Norman masonry and flat buttress may be seen running up
between the Perpendicular windows.

Besides, as already stated, in the neighbourhood of the rood-
loft, Norman shafts, once covered by the constructions appended
to that edifice, are still to be seen[k], and in like manner in the
southern side aisle part of the lower extremity of a Norman

---

[k] These Norman fragments are very
much out of the perpendicular, and appear
to indicate that the north side of the nave
was in a bad state of repair, which may
have occasioned the necessity for its rebuilding.

shaft appears, as shewn in the margin; this having been probably covered by some shrine or altar work.

From all these and similar appearances we are justified in saying that this part of the building was merely transformed, instead of being, as was the case with Canterbury nave, simply pulled down and rebuilt.

I mention the nave of Canterbury because there is a very singular resemblance between the history of the two naves. Comparing for example the compartment of Canterbury nave[1] with the compartment of Winchester nave shewn below in page 71, the general arrangement of the two compositions will be found the same. But the pier-arch moldings of the former are much lighter and the piers more slender than those of the latter. This is due to the different construction, the one having been completely rebuilt, the other being

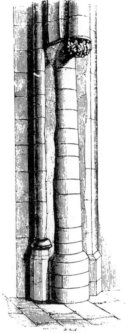

Fig. 34. Norman Shaft in South Aisle of Nave

a mere casing or refacing of a heavy Norman structure. So also the balcony of Winchester does not appear at Canterbury, and the panelling of the combined triforium and clerestory above, which in the former is set back in the middle and enriched with a frame of moldings, in the latter is all in one plane, because in the first case a thick Norman wall was to be dealt with and disguised. But the pattern of the tracery is the same in both examples, only that the Canterbury transom is higher in proportion. Also in both the opening of the triforium is pierced through the panel.

The side-aisle windows of Winchester are exactly the same as the clerestory windows. But in Canterbury the side-aisle windows differ totally from the clerestory windows, and the latter are the same as at Winchester. Now we have shewn that although the exact beginning of the rebuilding of Winchester nave is uncertain, yet that the parts in question, the compartments of the nave, are Wykeham's, and that he began his work in the November of 1394. There is every reason to

[1] Arch. History of Canterbury Cath.. p. 121.

suppose that the rebuilding of Canterbury nave was begun about 1380, or a little later; it went on slowly, and was not finished till the beginning of the fifteenth century[m]. The two works therefore went on together. But at Canterbury they began by pulling down the old nave. At Winchester Wykeham laid out a scheme, by which the pulling down of the old nave might be spared. Like all sanguine contrivers, he at first carried out his scheme too far, retaining even the Norman ashlaring at the lower part of the piers, and so setting out and designing his piers, that it was necessary merely to cut Perpendicular moldings upon the edge of the undisturbed Norman stones. Either this was found more troublesome than the making of new ones, on account of the bad state of the stone work and the necessity of replacing and patching, or else the contrast (still to be seen) between the small Norman stones and thick mortar beds, with the large close-jointed stones of the new work, was found too offensive. Certain it is that this part of the scheme was abandoned after the first eight piers to the west on the south side were completed[n]. The remainder of the piers on the south, and the whole of the piers on the north side of the nave, are cased with new ashlar from the pavement upwards. (It must be remembered that Wykeham's will has shewn us that he began his work on the south side.) By this time the Canterbury nave must have been carried up to the pier-arches, and as their clerestory was changed to a pattern resembling that of Winchester, while Winchester remained the same in side aisles and clerestory, it is fair to conclude that the first was copied from the last.

As to the lierne vaults which both examples are covered with, and the invention of which some have attributed to Wykeham, they were employed in Bishop Hotham's work at Ely, about the year 1336, and in Gloucester cathedral a few years earlier, namely, when Wykeham was about ten years old[o], not to mention their universal employment in Germany and other parts of the continent.

The plan of the pier of the nave (fig. 33.) will shew how small the difference is between its original state and the present, and how great was the skill that enabled the architect to trans-

---

[m] Arch. Hist. of Canterbury Cath., p. 118.

[n] In the general plan these piers are distinguished from the rest by being made wholly black.

[o] He was born in the year 1324, (Louth, 3.) .

form the heavy pier of the Norman work into a structure of so totally different a style. The lower or tinted half of this figure shews the pier as it stands, and below it is a profile of its arch-mold. But the upper half of the figure is double, and represents the present plan in comparison (by superposition) with the Norman pier. The difference between the two plans being tinted shews the portion of the old pier which was chipped away to convert it into the new one. The outlines which circumscribe both the upper half and the lower are the plans of the respective plinths ; the Norman plinth being as usual disposed in successive squares, and the Perpendicular one in successive portions of octagons, which are equiangular under shafts, and irregular under the intermediate moldings.

If the Norman pier of the nave, as shewn in this plan, be compared with that of the Norman transept already given in fig. 3, above, it will appear that with one exception they are alike. In fact, from I to D (the same letters are placed on corresponding parts in both figures), they are identical. But in the nave-pier an additional square edge C

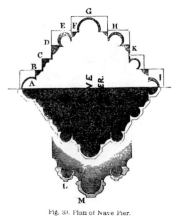

Fig. 38. Plan of Nave Pier.

is introduced, which does not appear in the transept. The shaft A and the square edge B behind it are the same in both.

The Norman pier consists of shafts A, E, G, H, K, and I, between which are placed square pier-edges as usual. In Wykeham's pier all that was done consisted in reducing the surface of the Norman shafts and adding moldings to the intermediate edges. The first was necessary because the Norman shafts are seldom upright, and their surface is not truly worked. This re-facing or re-working the masonry reduced the diameter of the shafts as shewn, and in addition to this the edge of each square was chamfered off and worked either into a casement or a swelled chamfer, as the figure shews. It is wonderful how completely these moldings have converted a pier so essentially Norman into one of so totally different a character[p].

In the western tower-piers (fig. 9. above,) the edges were also chamfered (as at K.) This will appear by comparing the group of shafts and pier edges at K with the similar group in its original state at P (in fig. 10.)

In fig. 34. the process of transformation is further illustrated by placing in juxtaposition an elevation of one compartment in its original Norman state, and an elevation of another in its present state. The Norman compartment is divided vertically into pier-arch, triforium, and clerestory, and these three members are nearly of equal altitude. The Norman shafts and capitals which still remain on the north side of the nave, where they were covered with the ancient rood-screen, shew that the pier-arches of the nave sprang from the same height as those of the transepts. Again the Norman main arch of the triforium still exists, as we shall presently see, in every compartment over the vault of the side aisles, by which it is proved that the triforium arch of the nave was at the same level within a few inches as that of the transepts.

Also the tops of the Norman shafts which separated the compartments are still to be seen over the vault of the nave, (fig. 31 above) exactly the same in form as those in the transepts.

These evidences make it certain that the nave was like the transepts in the general arrangement at least. Whether it had moldings added to it cannot be now ascertained, and if it had it would not vitiate the restoration in the figure, which is intended only to shew the general disposition and proportion of the composition.

The compartment of Wykeham's nave is divided into two parts vertically, instead of three; for although it has a triforium gallery, yet this is so completely subordinated to the clerestory window that it cannot be held as a separate division of the composition, as in the Norman work, where the triforium compartment is of equal importance and similar in its decoration to the other two, although not exactly like them. In Wykeham's work, on the contrary, we find above the lofty pier-arch what at first sight appears to be a clerestory window, divided at

[p] Britton's plate 3 contains a double plan somewhat similar to mine. But his plan assumes that the nave-pier was the same as that of the transept, overlooking the additional square edge C, so that the new pier, instead of being produced by a mere skinning of the old one, is made to project in front beyond it, which the Norman ashlaring that some of them retain shews not to have been the case.

Fig. 34. Compartment of Nave.

mid-height by a transom, and recessed under a deeply molded archway.   But it is above the transom only that the real window is formed, by glazing the spaces between the monials. Below the transom these spaces are filled with panels, and two narrow openings cut through the latter give access from the roof to a kind of balcony, which projects over the pier-arches. In each compartment this balcony exists, but there is no free passage from one to another ; to reach any one of them it is necessary to scramble over the tops of the vaults, at the risk of tumbling headlong into their pockets, as they are technically termed.   This mode of uniting the triforium and clerestory by the employment of a transom dividing the stone panels (or orbs) of the former from the glazed lights of the latter, is common enough at the period of Wykeham's work, and before it, but the balcony is unusual.

We have now to consider the process by which the Norman structure was converted into that which we have just described.

The pier-arch and mass of masonry, *B, C, D, E*, was entirely removed, leaving, however, the pier *A, B*, (shorn of its bases and capitals). Also the pillar *F* above, and the double arch *G*, which rested on it, was taken down.   The arch over this would of course remain, and indeed the back part of it does, to this day.   The clerestory arches and the window behind were also taken down, but the piers between were left standing, to the very top of the wall. It must be remembered that a Norman structure consists of a mere shell of wrought stonework or ashlaring, applied against a central mass or core of hard rubble work firmly compacted together, so firmly indeed that in most cases the ashlaring or skin, arch-voussoirs and all, may be entirely taken away and the rubble structure will stand firmly for ages.   Examples of this may often be seen in Norman ruins when the ashlaring has been stripped for building material, while the rubble has not been worth the labour of destruction.   Thus at Bury St. Edmund's, Thetford, Binham, Castle Acre, and in many other monastic ruins, Norman rubble walls still stand upright without a particle of ashlaring remaining. This process is assisted by the very slight bond which these rude workmen thought it necessary to establish between the skin and the body of the work, as well as by the superabundant and unnecessary strength which the enormous dimensions of their walls gave to the buildings, and which made them quite able to stand alone when they had lost their ashlar decoration. It is necessary fully to understand this before we can conceive the possibility of such changes as those which we have now to investigate.

I have shewn that the lower arches were cut away from between the piers, and the upper work also taken down, leaving only the separating piers themselves, which stood untouched from the pavement to the top of the wall, and connected by one range of the original arches only, namely, those of the triforium. Besides this, the ashlaring was stripped off the whole inner face of the rubble, with the exception of a small portion of pier below. The left hand portion of fig. 34 shews half of a compartment of the Norman work in this intermediate[q] state, as seen from the nave. On the other side of the pier the ashlaring was left undisturbed throughout the greatest part of it. Thus at the top the flat Norman buttress may still be seen on the leads under the clerestory, dividing the Perpendicular windows; and in the roof of the triforium, as already stated, the arches, $S\ T$, still remain, and are separated by the usual flat Norman buttress.

The portion of ashlaring on the outside of the piers at P, Q, R, which was allowed to remain, was wrought into Perpendicular moldings, a process which was comparatively easy, because, as I have shewn, the plan of the new pier was very little different from that of the old one. However, in the later parts of the work this small portion of the original ashlar was entirely removed, as I have already explained.

The eastern extremities of the side aisles of the nave, as seen in the transepts, illustrate this process of transformation very completely. One of these compartments is shewn in the elevation fig. 1 above, at E, G, F, H. The lower part has undergone the process of conversion from Norman to Perpendicular. The upper half remains in its original state. Fig. 35 is a view of the same two compartments of the triforium. But this view is taken from within, the artist standing upon the undulated upper surface of the vault of Wykeham's side aisle. The right hand compartment of the triforium

---

[q] For the sake of illustration, I have represented the building in its intermediate state, completely stripped, thus shewing how much of the old was retained. But in the actual process the ashlaring was probably taken off and replaced in small portions at a time, so that no compartment of the building ever appeared at any one moment in the state here represented.

retains its Norman double sub-arching; but in the left compartment the double sub-arch has been removed, as well as its central pillar. Wykeham's pier-arch and vault rises high above the original floor of the triforium, and his balcony appears nearly covering the front of the original triforium arch. The Norman shaft and capital that carried the sub-arch may be seen half absorbed in the new masonry.

Fig. 35. View from the Roof.

I have said that the design of the Norman nave was essentially the same as that of the transepts, with one difference, which I shall now explain more minutely. Comparing the two piers, fig. 3 and fig. 33, I have shewn that the pier of the nave has one member in addition, namely, a square edge C, next to the nave. As this square edge (now decorated with a swelled chamfer) lies on that part of the Norman ashlaring that runs up the middle of the pier as high as P (fig. 34), instead of stopping at Q, it could not have belonged to the pier-arch shafts. Also the remaining Norman shafts at the top of the wall (L, K, fig. 34, and fig. 31) shew that no additional edge was present there. Hence I infer that this edge was disposed of as I have shewn in the elevation, namely, that it carried an arch over the triforium. A similar arrangement is to be found elsewhere, as for example at Norwich and at Romsey. The shafts L, K, are not to be found in every compartment. If the piers of the nave be numbered from the west end, calling the half pier 1, it will be observed that these shafts only run up to the roof over piers

2, 4, 6, 8, 10, 11, 12. These piers are marked in the general plan with $O.^r$ They are in fact alternately disposed in the western part of the nave, but are given to every pier in the eastern part, extending as far as the steps to the choir. As the part of the church which contains the choir was probably built first, and the rest of the nave afterwards, it is not surprising to find such a change of plan; indeed, this is very commonly the case. In my elevation of the original state (fig. 34) I have shewn one pier running up (as at L, K,) and the next stopping short at M; and farther, I have supposed the clerestory above to follow the same design as that of the transepts over the pier, which, like the one in question, stops short (at D, fig. 1).

The monuments in this cathedral consist of a very fine series of chantry chapels, beginning with that of Bishop Edingdon, and ending with Bishop Gardiner. As it forms no part of my plan to describe these, which, indeed, could only be done by the help of elaborate engravings, I shall content myself with inserting their dates in the following list of the dated examples of architecture, with which I conclude this essay on Winchester cathedral.

[r] This remark applies to the piers on the north as well as on the south side, although the reference is only marked on the latter in the plan.

ARCH-MOLDS.

W. & S. dd

INCHES.

A. Arcade on the ground, in De Lucy's Aisles.
B. Arcade of the Trefoil-arches at the upper part of the wall of the Lady Chapel.
C. Pier-arches of De Lucy's Aisles.
D. Arch between these Aisles and their Eastern Chapels.
E. Eastern Arches of the Presbytery.   (AB, CD, Fig. 19.)
F. North-eastern Arch of do   (GK, Fig. 19.)
G. South-eastern do.   (FM, Fig. 19.)
H. The remaining Arches of the Presbytery.   (KL, MN &c. Fig. 19.)
I. Arch of the Western Porch.

N.B.—The Pier-arch of the Nave is shewn in Fig. 33.

CAPITALS AND BASES.

The same letters of reference are employed in the corresponding figures.

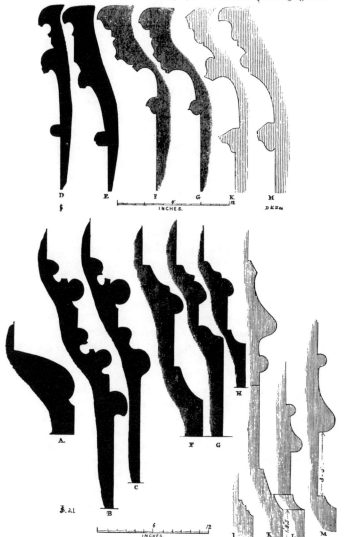

A. Base of Norman Shaft, remaining in Gardner's Chantry. (at V, Fig. 36.)
B. Respond Pier of De Lucy's Work.
C. Central Piers of do.
D, E. Lady Chapel.
F. Piers of the Presbytery.
G. North-east Pier of Presbytery. (K, Fig. 19.)
H. Eastern Piers of the Presbytery. (A, B, D, Fig. 19.)
I. Edingdon's Work in the Nave.   K. Nave Pier.
L. Side Aisle of Nave.   M. Side Aisle of Presbytery.

THE parts of the cathedral are represented in block merely, that is to say, each pier, instead of being laid down with all its shafts and moldings, is represented as a simple mass bounded by straight lines which follow, or rather circumscribe, the general outline. The windows also are omitted. Thus the appearance of the plan is simplified. The different periods of the work are indicated by different tints of shading. Their history has been minutely investigated in the preceding pages, by comparing the records with the building, but unfortunately much of it rests upon induction. The results to which I have arrived may be summed up as follows:—(1.) The complete Norman cathedral was erected by Walkelin; commenced in 1079, and so far completed in 1093 that the monks entered it. Of this building the transepts remain; the plan of its east end is preserved in its crypt, and the extent and plan of its western portion shewn in the masonry concealed behind and within Wykeham's work, and by the foundations lately exposed in front of the present building and shewn in this plan. The transepts, however, were erected with changes of plan, explained in the second chapter. (2.) The tower fell in 1107. The piers of the present tower, and the four in immediate connection with them in the transepts, are the result of this event. (3.) De Lucy's work was begun in 1202 in the Early English style. The outside wall was first erected, without disturbing the Norman Lady Chapel. Then this Lady Chapel and the circular aisle and towers of the great apse were taken down, and the piers and vault of the new work erected. (4.) The apse itself was taken down and the present polygonal Decorated termination substituted, apparently about 1320. Of this work only the north arch and the eastern arches remain; the north arch is later in style and differently connected with De Lucy's work. (5.) The Norman clerestory and triforium of the remainder of the presbytery, namely, between the apse and the tower, were next taken down, about 1350, under Edingdon, and their Norman side-aisles still remaining, the masonry in front of them was so far reduced as to allow the present piers, arches, and clerestory to be erected in front. The arrangement of these, being copied from the eastern compartment, appears rather earlier than its moldings and windows. On the other hand, the tracery of the clerestory windows of this presbytery, which belongs to the second period, was also inserted into the eastern compartments, and thus on the whole it happens that these windows appear later than the design of the presbytery. (6.) The further progress of the presbytery was abandoned, and the west end of the nave taken down by Edingdon before 1366 (the year of his death.) His work consists of the present west end with its great window, and of the north and south outer wall of the side-aisle, including one and two compartments respectively, as shewn by the different tint in the plan. (7.) The complete transformation of the nave was begun in 1394, by Wykeham on the south side, left incomplete at his death in 1404, and finished by his successors. (8.) The Lady Chapel was lengthened eastward by Priors Hunton and Silkstede, between 1470 and 1524. (9.) The Norman side-aisles of the presbytery were taken down and replaced by the present ones, in imitation of Wykeham's aisles in the nave, by Bishop Fox and Prior Silkstede, between 1500 and 1528. The side screens of the presbytery were also erected in 1524.

The smaller dated works are the chantries, which were probably erected during the life of the persons by whom they were founded. This is recorded in the case of Wykeham, in his will.

Reference
to Plan

(4) Edingdon's Chantry	.	.	.	1345 to 1366
(1) Wykeham's Chantry	.	.	.	1367 to 1404
(11) Beaufort's Chantry	.	.	.	1405 to 1447
(10) Waynflete's Chantry	.	.	.	1447 to 1486
(0) Langton's Chantry	.	.	.	1493 to 1500
(9) Fox's Chantry	.	.	.	1500 to 1528
(8) Gardiner's Chantry	.	.	.	1531 to 1555

Silkstede's Chapel in south transept, and (5) Pulpit in choir 1498 to 1524

LIST OF ENGRAVINGS.

Fig. 36   HISTORICAL BLOCK PLAN OF WINCHESTER CATHEDRAL.

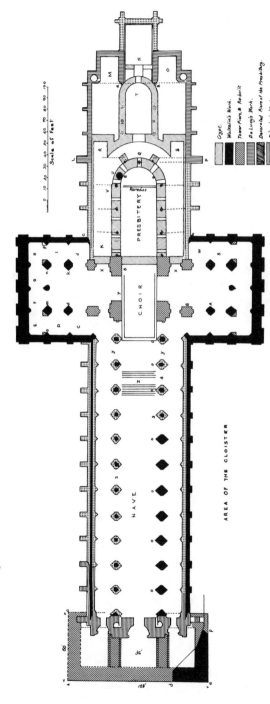

The original colour legend has been replaced by the shading scheme